The Howells
of New Jersey, Virginia, Ohio
and Points West

By
Richard E. Wallace
Robert W. Cameron
Carmen J. Finley

1994

Published 1994 By

HERITAGE BOOKS, INC.
1540-E Pointer Ridge Place, Bowie, Md., 20716
(301) 390-7709

ISBN 0-7884-0052-5

A Complete Catalog Listing Hundreds of Titles On
Genealogy, History, and Americana
Available Free Upon Request

TABLE OF CONTENTS

PICTURES

TABLES

APPENDIX A - TRANSCRIBED DOCUMENTS

APPENDIX B - 1850 CENSUS RECORDS

FOREWORD

This book about Hugh and Margaret Howell and some of their descendants has a history all its own. It can probably be dated to 1955 when I, in a 10th grade biology class, was given an assignment to prepare a family pedigree chart. This assignment, which was completed based on family records and conversations with older family members, stirred an interest in family history that has lasted to the present day.

The foregoing does not mean that I became a full fledged genealogist over night. Far from it. Other priorities and interests kept family history in the background for a long time - tucked away but not forgotten. It was not until after the very successful TV series, "Roots," that I started to search seriously for family ancestors, including the Howells. This was in 1978. Then I began to learn about the nuts and bolts of the genealogist's craft: family records, vital records, probate records, and census records, to name a few. I also learned that if you are a descendant of a typical American family, which most of us are, you had better be prepared for years of patient research, punctuated by moments of pure joy when a newly found piece of evidence proves a long-held hypothesis. In other words, the easily intimidated or frustrated had better look elsewhere for entertainment.

One of the first family lines I attempted to trace belonged to my grandmother, Myrtle (Howell) Wallace. From the earlier conversations with her, I knew that her maiden name was Howell and that her parents were Chalmers H. Howell and Marinda Worthen. I didn't know much else about them, but I did know who most of their children were. Their names were recorded on my old 13-foot pedigree chart, known around the Wallace household as the "Dead Sea Scroll." From this small beginning eventually came the rest of the material found in this book.

I think the first record I requested was C.H. Howell's 1921 death record. When this record arrived, it gave me his parents' names and the fact that he had been born in New Concord, Ohio. Research in Ohio records led to other Howell names, in particular an Abner, who appeared to be the father of many of the younger Howells in Muskingum County, Ohio. Then a problem developed, the type of problem that has stopped cold many a budding genealogist. I had found circumstantial evidence that Madison Howell, Chalmers' father, could be the son of Abner Howell, but I could not find primary evidence to support my strong belief that he actually was. This inability to find primary evidence, sometimes referred to as the "stone wall," stalled my Howell research for over five years. Without a proven link, it is not possible to realistically carry research back into earlier generations.

It was at this time, in 1989, that I had the good fortune to meet, through correspondence, Robert W. Cameron and Carmen J. Finley. These two very capable individuals helped prove that Madison was indeed Abner's son. With this added information, and much more, our joint research carried the family line back another two generations, to Virginia and New Jersey. Prior to our meeting, Carmen and Bob had pursued their own independent research of the Howell family, which had led them to the same Abner Howell in which I was interested. A few words about these co-authors, plus a few about myself, are in order.

Robert Cameron, my 4th cousin, is a retired Mechanical engineer with a degree from the University of Illinois at Champaign-Urbana. He served in the United States Army Air Corps during World War II, with the rank of 1st Lieutenant. After the war, he worked as an engineer for the Timken Company in Canton, Ohio, retiring in 1985. While at Timken, he was granted four patents related to his work. Another memorable achievement while there was his responsibility for the selection and application of the bearings to be used in the landing wheels of the Space Shuttle. The bearings, which were limited in size by design specifications, were required to operate subjected to high accelerations under extremely heavy loads. Through the use of a combination of several application innovations, the bearings have performed perfectly. Bob makes his home in Canton, Ohio.

Dr. Carmen J. Finley of Santa Rosa, California, a retired research psychologist and good friend of another Howell cousin, has been actively engaged in genealogical research since 1979. She is a past president of the Sonoma County Genealogical Society and is currently serving again as Vice-President and Program Chairman. She is also currently the Chairman of the National Genealogical Society's Family History Writing Contest. She has been publishing articles since 1988. They have appeared in the National Genealogical Society Quarterly, The American Genealogist, The Virginia Genealogist, and Tennessee Ancestors. One of these included the knotty problem of straightening out the family of Abner Howell of Muskingum County:

Carmen J. Finley, "Howells of Muskingum County, Ohio: Correlating and Interpreting Evidence to Reconstruct a Family," National Genealogical Society Quarterly, 80 (Sept. 1992) 194-203.

As for me, I have just completed my 31st year with the Social Security Administration in Kansas City. I am on the personal staff of the Regional Commissioner, specializing in retirement claims policy. I interpret and clarify policy for the 77 offices in the four state region served by Kansas City. I have been involved in genealogical research since 1978. I have had several articles on genealogy published as follows:

Richard E. Wallace, "George Dement Robey/Roby, A Lincoln County, North Carolina Pioneer," Bulletin of The Genealogical Society of Old Tryon County, xix (May 1991, No. 2), 81-84.

Richard E. Wallace, "More Robey Family Notes," Bulletin of The Genealogical Society of Old Tryon County, xix (Nov. 1991, No. 4), 165-167.

Richard E. Wallace, "William Cornelius of Lincoln County, NC and Some of his Descendants," Bulletin of The Genealogical Society of Old Tryon County, xx (Nov. 1992, No. 4) 166-172.

A book like ours is the product of many hands. Much of the material in it came about through the efforts of individuals who live at or near the places where the Howells lived in the 18th and 19th centuries. The authors would like to acknowledge the fine help provided by these individuals, including the courthouse staffs of several counties where our Howell ancestors lived. Even when they couldn't help personally, courthouse staffs were almost always willing to furnish names of local research genealogists who could help. The Probate Court staff in Guernsey County, Ohio went out of their way to help us.

Research in New Jersey, the early home of Hugh Howell, was aided by the research efforts of Roxanne Carkhuff, P.O. Box 334, Ringoes, NJ 08551; Virginia Brown, P.O. Box 118, Titusville, NJ 08560; and Fred Sisser III, Box 6493, Bridgewater, NJ 08807.

Howell research in Virginia was greatly aided by the work of Theresa Dye, 1 Donn Ave., Berryville, VA 22611. Ms. Dye treated the Howells almost as if they were her own family. She not only came up with good records,she also did a fine job in analyzing her findings, putting them into historical perspective, etc. We would also like to recognize the work of Phyllis T. Scott, 6449 Rattle Branch Rd., Marshall, VA 22115 and Dottie Kessler, P.O. Box 67, Fincastle, VA 24090. These fine researchers helped us try to learn more about some of Hugh Howell's children and grandchildren in Virginia.

Special thanks go to Ohio researcher Sylvia Hargrove, 27 W. Overlook Dr., Zanesville, OH 43201, Hilda Yinger, 2740 Adamsville Rd., Zanesville, OH 43701 and Carolyn Z. Wolf, 339 Guilford Ave., Woodsfield, OH 43793 for the work they did. Of this group, we probably corresponded more with Ms. Yinger, than with the other two. Hilda always responded to the many letters we sent her, even when we suspected she might be getting a little tired of our requests for still more information. That we have singled Hilda out by no means diminishes the efforts of Hargrove and Wolf.

A special thanks goes to Mrs. Mae Morris, 7145 Plainfield Road, Kimbolton, Ohio 43749. Mrs Morris, nee Viola Mae Kennedy, is a

4th great granddaughter of Hugh Howell. She willingly loaned the family bible of Abner[4] Howell to the authors to enable them to document important data on the family of Abner[3] Howell.

I would like to thank my cousin, Harriett Campbell, for providing data on her mother's family and the family of Chalmers Howell. Her correspondence also provides an important reminder for genealogists. Don't put off talking to older generation relatives before it's too late. Only days after Harriett secured data from Aunt Grace, Myrtle (Howell) Wallace's half-sister, Grace died suddenly of a heart attack.

The history of our ancestors, unless we happen to tap into a "famous" one, is reconstructed from the records they leave behind. Primary records, those closest to the time of the event and recorded by someone involved in the event, are the best sources. Secondary sources such as biographical sketches, genealogies written by other persons, local histories and the like, may be helpful, but some are prone to error. We have tried to rely as much as possible on primary records, but have filled in with secondary records where otherwise there would be gaps. We think the conclusions in this book will stand the test of time in nearly all cases. If a few don't, it won't be for lack of trying. We think researchers of this branch of the Howell family now have a well-documented base upon which they might wish to build their own personal stories. After nearly 300 years, Hugh and Margaret's descendants must number in the hundreds of thousands by now. We have only touched on a few of those many descendants.

Richard E. Wallace
Overland Park, KS 66212
September 1993

CHAPTER ONE

WELSH ORIGINS

The surname Howell has both Welsh and English origins.[1] The Welsh version comes from the personal name *Hywel,* meaning eminent, popular since the Middle Ages in honor of a 10th century law-giving king. The English version is a place name in Lincolnshire. In old English it was called *Hun Wella,* meaning "the stream of the cubs." Eventually the name evolved into the current rendition.

Spelling of the Howell name in the records the authors have examined for this work have been fairly consistent, HOWELL being the predominant version. Variant spellings that have been found are Howel, Howells, Howill, and a few Howles.

Primary proof has not been found that the Loudoun County Howells originally came from Wales, but there are some clues that they might have been. Other Howells (not necessarily related) who lived in close proximity to them in New Jersey were Welsh descendants. A direct descendant of Hugh Howell, our primary ancestor, recalls her mother telling her that their family was originally from Wales.

Every student of American history has read about the colonial experience, the hard-won struggle for independence from Britain, and then the subsequent territorial expansion with its westward migration of thousands of settlers. As readers will soon see, Howells of this book were every bit a part of this experience. Their story begins in colonial New Jersey in the early 1700s where Hugh Howell probably farmed rented land. During the 1760s, the family moved to northern

---

[1] Patrick Hanks & Flavia Hodges, <u>A Dictionary of Surnames</u> (New York: Oxford University Press, 1988), p. 266.

Virginia where they were finally able to buy their own small parcels of land.   Shortly after 1800, family members started on the move again - this time to eastern Ohio, a new state where land was plentiful and cheap.

Ohio proved to be a staging area for further migration by Howell family members.   After the middle of the 19th century, some of Hugh's great grandchildren can be found in Missouri and Kansas. Later generations proceeded on to Colorado and then on to California.

CHAPTER TWO

NEW JERSEY AND VIRGINIA
HUGH HOWELL - GENERATION ONE

Our research on Hugh Howell reveals that he was born about 1720, possibly in New Jersey. He died in the spring of 1777 in Loudoun County, Virginia. He married Margaret _____ before 1745, probably in New Jersey. She was born before 1730. She died in the 5-year period ending 1799, most likely in Loudoun County. Parentage for Hugh and Margaret has not been established by primary documents, but some researchers have drawn their own conclusion on this subject.

A Howell file in the Hunterdon County, New Jersey Historical Society, Flemington, contains some very specific conclusions about Hugh Howell, his father, his wife, and his brother.[2] According to this file, an older Hugh Howell was born 17 April 1659 in Wales, and he emigrated to America in 1699. He supposedly died 14 September 1745 in Sussex County, New Jersey. He is said to be the father of Hugh Howell, born 1720. The younger Hugh allegedly married a Margaret Hixon and died years later in 1777. His brother, stated to be a Sampson Howell, was born 17 December 1717 in Sussex County. At that time, Sussex County was part of Hunterdon County.

In light of the very specific information in the Historical Society file, the authors tried very hard to verify it. The Historical Society file does not contain the documentation to support the conclusions that had been made by an earlier researcher. This effort has established that the younger Hugh Howell did live in New Jersey, did have a wife

---

[2] Roxanne K. Carkhuff, P.O. Box 334, Ringoes, NJ 08551 to Richard Wallace, 15 April 1991. Original in possession of author Wallace.

named Margaret, and did die in 1777. These statements will be documented in the paragraphs that follow.

What has not been established is that Hugh Howell was the son of the older Hugh Howell or any other Howell, or that he had a brother named Sampson. The maiden name of his wife has not been proved to be Hixon, but readers will soon see that there has been a close connection between the Howell and Hixon families. Numerous records were searched to prove the Hugh/Hugh connection, including colonial New Jersey deeds and abstracts of New Jersey wills from 1670-1800. So far this research has not produced the desired results. Neither has a marriage record for Hugh and Margaret been located in New Jersey.

The 1699 emigration date has not been verified either, but an early New Jersey reference to a Hugh Howell can be found in the 1705 deed from a John Holcombe's land.[3] The deed describes the land "as beginning at ye uppermost corner of ye lands formerly Hugh Howells, now Robert Eatons on the Delaware River side ... " No trace of possession by Hugh Howell is available except in the wording of the Holcombe deed. One researcher the authors hired suggested the absence of land records for the various Hugh Howells is that they might have leased land and did not own any outright. This might explain the fact that deeds in their names have not been found.[4]

The Hunterdon County Loan Office Records contain a reference to a Hugh Howell.[5] The actual loan was taken out 30 April 1733 by a Thomas Hunt for a tract of land in Amwell Township bounded on the east by Hugh Howell.

---

[3] A Collection of Papers Read Before the Bucks County Historical Society, V (N.p.: Fackenthal Publication Fund, 1926), p. 599.

[4] Virginia A. Brown, P.O. Box 118, Titusville, NJ 08560 to Richard Wallace, December 1991. Original in possession of author Wallace.

[5] Hunterdon County, NJ, Loan Office Records, #36.

The September 1743 inventory of John Holcombe's estate, which was settled in Hunterdon County, firms up the relationship between Hugh Howell, Sr. and Sampson Howell.[6] Wording in this document refers to the debt due the estate by Hugh Howell and son Sampson. This is the same John Holcombe who acquired land in 1705. John Holcolmbe lived in Amwell, Hunterdon County, where he was a large landowner and member of The Society of Friends.[7]

On 2 April 1744, James Howell and Henry Oxley signed for a mortgage deed on 150 acres of land in Hunterdon County, Amwell Township, "excepting thereto two and a half acres sold to Thomas Howell, John Howell, John Evans and Daniel Geano, Junr. and Hugh Howell."[8] Researcher Carkhuff suggested that the excepted acreage was a lot set aside for the development of a new church in the area.

The town records of Hopewell, New Jersey provide information on the younger Hugh Howell and other families with whom he associated. These records provide abstracts of the Town Book - officers, meetings and estrays. They also contain abstracts of the records of the Old School Baptist Church - baptisms, dismissals, deaths, marriages and excommunications.

The town records show that on 11 March 1746/7, Hue Howell was elected overseer of highways, "over brook below."[9] The records also show that Matthew Hixson was selected "Overseer of Road" above

---

[6] A. Van Doren Honeyman, ed., Calendar of New Jersey Wills and Administrations, 1731-1750, II (Somerville, NJ: The Unionist-Gazette Assn., 1918), p. 241.

[7] William W.H. Davis, Genealogical History of Bucks County (Baltimore, MD: Genealogical Publishing, reprinted 1975), p. 608.

[8] Hunterdon County, NJ, Loan Office Records, #193.

[9] Lida Cokefair Gedney, comp., The Town Records of Hopewell, New Jersey, Board of Managers of the New Jersey Society of the Colonial Dames of America (New York: Little, Ives, 1931), p. 23.

*Hopewell New Jersey First Baptist Church (Old School). Hugh
and Margaret Howell were baptized in the old stone church
which was replaced in 1822 by the one shown here.*

Stony Brook.[10] The date of his selection was 1742/43.

The records of the Old School Baptist Church show that Hugh Howell
was received as a member by baptism on 11 November 1747.
"Margret" Howell was baptized 18 June 1748. She was dismissed by
1749.[11]

---

[10] Ibid., p. 21.

[11] Ibid., p. 131.

Ketoctin Church, Shelburne Parish, Loudoun County, Virginia. The Howells, the Hixsons and Deacon Henry Oxley and family relocated here in the 1760s.

Henry Oxley was a deacon in the Old School Baptist Church.[12] On 19 April 1761, Henry Oxley and his daughters, Hannah and Rachel, were dismissed to "Catoctan" Church in Virginia.[13] The Ketoctin Church was located in Loudoun County, Virginia.

Also belonging to the Old School Baptist Church were members of the Hixon family, including Timothy Hixon and his wife, Rachel. On 27

---

[12] Ibid., p. 130.

[13] Ibid., p. 133.

October 1765, Timothy Hixon and wife were dismissed to "Catoctan" in Virginia.[14]

The Stout family was instrumental in organizing the First Baptist Church (Old School) of Hopewell in 1715.[15] After its organization, meetings were held in private homes, and for a number of years the congregation had no regular minister. John Hart donated land for the building of a church, and this construction was done in 1747. The Rev. Isaac Eaton became the regular minister in 1748. The old stone church was torn down in 1822, to be replaced by the brick building pictured here.

Apparently Hugh and Margaret Howell were members of the Old School Church for only a short time, as Margaret was dismissed in 1749. The church records do not show it, but Hugh and his wife also left New Jersey for Loudoun County, Virginia. The time of their departure for Virginia can be determined from their son's Revolutionary War pension application. On 15 August 1832 Reuben Howell swore in a court held in Columbiana County, Ohio he was born 26 February 1762 near Trenton, New Jersey. He went on to say that "at the age of about 15 months my father moved to Loudoun County - state of Virginia."[16] Reuben's statement places the family's move to Virginia in May or June 1763.

The Miscellaneous Court Records of Hunterdon County contain five references to Hugh Howell for the year 1763.[17] The references concern the debts of Timothy Coalman and William Sherd. All debts

---

[14] Ibid., p. 135.

[15] Alice B. Lewis, Hopewell Valley Heritage (Hopewell, NJ: Hopewell Museum, 1973), pp. 8-9.

[16] Revolutionary War Pension File for Reuben Howell (S2327), National Archives Microfilm M804, Roll 1347.

[17] Index to Miscellaneous Court Records, Hunterdon County, NJ, items 6406, 6446, 29494, 8792, 14596.

are in the amount of £100. Hugh was probably trying to clear up accounts before leaving for Virginia permanently.

Although Hugh moved his family permanently to Loudoun County, Virginia in 1763, his own presence in the area can be dated to 1762. The 1762 Loudoun County Tithable List gives us a picture of the Howells living there.[18] This list, which was used for tax purposes, enumerates the head of households and all males age 16 and above. Thus everyone on this list was born on or before 1746.

In 1762, there were four separate Howell households in Loudoun County. These are listed below, along with the other tithables that lived there. The names, some spelled Howel, were taken from James Hamilton's list.

> Timothy Howel, Danl. Howel, Abner Howel
> John Howell, Hezekiah Howell
> John Howel
> Hugh Howel, Wm. Howel

Hugh is not found in the list for 1764 (1763 is not available). Only John "Howill" is listed that year.[19] Hugh and William reappear in the 1765 List in separate households.[20] Hugh is listed as having 125 acres. Most of the other Howells found in the 1762 List can also be found in the 1765 List.

After arriving in Loudoun County, Virginia, Hugh Howell obtained a deed 17 May 1764 on a 125 acre tract of land along Catoctin Creek.[21] His land bordered the property of William Hoge, John Hough and Matthew Hixon. The deed was signed in the presence of

---

[18] Ruth and Sam Sparacio eds., <u>Tithables Loudoun County, Virginia 1758-1769</u> (McLean, VA: Antient Press, 1991), pp. 17-18.

[19] Ibid., p. 26.

[20] Ibid., p. 30.

[21] Loudoun County, VA, Deed Bk D:241.

Timothy, John and Abner Howell. This land would remain in Hugh's hands for the rest of his life.

In 1771, there were eight separate Howell households in Loudoun County, all in Shelburne Parish.[22] Geographically this parish constituted the western half of the county, bounded on the east by Goose Creek, on the west by the Blue Ridge Mountains, and on the south by the Fauquier County line. These households are listed below, along with the other tithables that lived there. This list enumerates the heads of household and all males age 16 and above. Thus everyone on this list was born on or before 1755.

Abner Howel, Archibald McNail
William Howell
Hugh Howell, Andrew Howell, Benj. Howell
John Howell, Hizekiah Howell
Charles Howell
Timothy Howell, Thomas Howell, David Howell
John Howell's
John Howell

Four Hixon families were also living in Shelburne Parish in 1771.[23] These were Matthew Hixon, William Hixon, Daniel Hixon, and Timothy Hixon. Each family had only one male age 16 or older.

The Henry Oxley, who had been dismissed to "Catoctan" in 1761, can also be found in the 1771 Tithable List.[24] He is listed in the household of Clare Oxley. On the same page is found a Harry Oxley, Jur.

---

[22] Pollyanna Creekmore, "Loudoun County, Virginia 1771 Tithable List," Virginia Genealogist 16 (Oct.-Dec., 1972), p. 244, 17 (Jan.-Mar., 1973), p. 11.

[23] Ibid., 17 (Jan.-Mar., 1973), p. 11.

[24] Ibid., 17 (Jan.-Mar., 1973), p. 107.

On 9 April 1774, Matthew Hixon deeded 217 acres of land to his son, William Hixon. On the same day, he deeded 247 acres of land to another son, Timothy Hixon. Witnesses to these transactions were Hugh (his mark) Howell, Joseph Bonham and Charles Howell.[25] When Matthew bought this 464 acres of land in 1764, the description of the land mentioned "corner to Hugh Howell."[26] The earlier transaction was signed in the presence of Timothy Howell, John Howell, and Abner Howell.

We are fortunate that Hugh Howell made a will that identifies his wife and his children. Sensing that his time was near, he prepared a will 6 March 1777.[27] In it he stated that he was a farmer and was "very sick and weak in body." He mentioned his "well beloved" wife, Margaret, and granted her "his land together with all my moveable estate as long as she remains my widow during her natural life." After her death he stipulated that the land and moveable estate should be sold and jointly divided among all his children.

The children named in Hugh's will were Andrew, Abner, John, Benjamin, Daniel, Reuben, Rachel and Ann Howell. We already had clues to the older sons from the 1771 Tithable List. Hugh followed the customary practice of naming his oldest son, William, executor along with Timothy Hixon, who is also probably a close relative. Hugh signed his will by mark (H). Witnesses were Francis Hague, William Hixon and Timothy Hixon.

Hugh Howell died sometime after 6 March 1777 and before 12 May 1777, when his will was filed for probate. William Howell and Timothy Hixon came forward and qualified to be executors of the estate.

---

[25] Ruth and Sam Sparacio, eds., <u>Deed Abstracts of Loudoun County, Virginia:</u> <u>1774-1775</u> (McLean, VA: Antient Press, 1990), pp. 28-29.

[26] Ruth and Sam Sparacio, eds., <u>Deed Abstracts of Loudoun County, Virginia:</u> <u>1762-1765</u> (McLean, VA: Antient Press, 1987), pp. 52-53.

[27] Loudoun County, VA, Will Bk B:176.

After Hugh's death, Margaret remained on the farm that was left to her during her lifetime. She did not remarry as some researchers have suggested. After Hugh's death, she continued to be listed on the personal property tax rolls as Margaret Howell. In 1785, her name appears as "Margrett" Howell.[28] Listed with her were sons "Ruben" and Benjamin. That year she was taxed on three horses and seven cattle.

One persistent myth we would like to dispel is that Margaret Howell subsequently married Timothy Hixon, the co-executor of Hugh Howell's estate. We don't know when or where this story originated, but one genealogy of the Hixon family concludes that Timothy's third wife was Margaret Patterson and that "Margaret may have been the widow of Hugh Howell ...".[29]

Timothy Hixon did marry a woman named Margaret, who is mentioned by name in his 1811 Loudoun County will.[30] He also listed 14 children, including Flemon Hixon, a child stated to be under age 21.

Margaret Hixon survived her husband by about 10 years. She died in 1821 and is buried in the graveyard of the Fairfax Meeting House.[31] She had prepared her will in 1818, in which she stated that Flemon, her son, was not age 21.[32] In the event of Flemon's death without issue, she made provision for the children of her deceased sister, Jane

---

[28] Loudoun County Personal Property Tax List (1785), Part 1: 1782-1787, Battalion 1, N. pag., microfilmed by Virginia State Library, Richmond, VA. Copy available at Thomas Balch Library, Local History Room, Leesburg, VA.

[29] William A. Sausaman, Ten Generations of Hixons in America (1686-1976) (Springfield, IL: author, 1977), p. 5.

[30] Loudoun County, VA, Will Bk K:89.

[31] Tombstone inscription for M. Hixon, Fairfax Meeting House Cemetery, Waterford, VA.

[32] Loudoun County, VA, Will Bk N:338.

Rodgers, "excepting her son Flemon Rodgers to have no part thereof, as he has been provided for by Flemon Patterson ...".

Taking the documents we have already described, and combining them with the following statements from a California researcher of the Hixon family, readers can see that Margaret Howell did not marry Timothy Hixon. Actually he married Margaret Wilson/Patterson (1763-1821),[33] daughter of Mary Wilson. She was raised by the Fleming Patterson family of Loudoun and Fairfax County, Virginia. According to Ms Sechrist, Fleming Patterson died about 1815 and made provisions in his will for Flemon Hixon and Flemon Rodgers.

Finally, if we stop to consider when Margaret Howell had to have been born (before 1730), she could not have been the mother of a child who was born around 1800.

Margaret Howell continues to appear in the personal property tax rolls until 1795[34] when it no longer appears. This absence could approximate the time of her death since no other record of that event has been found. She also could have gone to live with another family in the area. In any event, she was more than likely dead by 1799.

On 9 December 1799, the executors of Hugh Howell's estate sold the approximately 126 acres that had been purchased in 1764 to Conrad Virts for the sum of "£507 good and lawful money of Virginia."[35] The transaction was signed by Timothy Hixon and William Howell.

The accounting of Hugh Howell's estate took place 14 May 1804.[36] The estate had a final value of a little more than £559. Most of this value came from the land sale in 1799. Legatees mentioned by name

---

[33] Carol Sechrist, Los Angeles, CA to Robert Cameron 17 November 1992, copies in possession of authors.

[34] Loudoun County Personal Property Tax List, (1787-1797), Part 2.

[35] Loudoun County, VA, Deed Bk Z:418.

[36] Loudoun County, VA, Will Bk G:217.

in the accounting were William Howell, Ruben Howell, Abner Howell/Abner's estate, Benjamin Howell and Rachel Howell.

Getting back to some of the unresolved problems mentioned earlier, we don't know who Hugh Howell's parents were or when or where he was born. The alleged 1720 birth date is not unreasonable when we consider the ages of his children. We don't know when Margaret was born either, but a birth date in the 10-year period ending 1730 would not be out of line for her. Based on the interaction between the Howells and Hixons in New Jersey and Virginia, it can be seen how some researchers have concluded that her maiden name was Hixon. As stated earlier, this name has not yet been proven.

The children of Hugh and Margaret Howell have been identified from his 1777 will. Their names will be restated, along with their actual or approximate dates of birth and their birth places.

+2	i.	William[2] Howell, born about 1745, in New Jersey. *Stayed in London Co., VA d. 1817*
+3	iii.	Andrew Howell, born about 1753, in New Jersey.
+4	iii.	John Howell, born about 1753, in New Jersey.
+5	iv.	Abner Howell, born before 1755, in New Jersey.
+6	v.	Benjamin Howell, born about 1755, in New Jersey. *Went to Ohio*
+7	vi.	Daniel Howell, born about 1757, in New Jersey.
+8	vii.	Reuben Howell, born 26 February 1762, near Trenton, New Jersey. *Went to Ohio*
+9	viii.	Rachel Howell, born before March 1777, in New Jersey or Virginia.
+10	ix.	Ann Howell, born before March 1777, in New Jersey or Virginia.

CHAPTER THREE

HUGH HOWELL'S CHILDREN: BEGINNING THE MOVE
TO OHIO
GENERATION TWO

Because of the numerous Howell families found in the vicinity of Hugh Howell and the common given names used by different Howell families, not all of Hugh's children could be positively identified. However, of the three who could be positively identified, one (William) lived out his life in Virginia. Two (Benjamin and Reuben), moved on to Ohio. While only William and Reuben could be identified as Revolutionary War soldiers, it is likely there were others as their estimated birth dates would have made most of the males eligible to have served.

2. William[2] Howell (Hugh[1]) was born about 1745[37] probably in New Jersey,[38] and died 4 April 1817 in Loudoun County, Virginia.[39] He married Martha Marks, daughter of John and Ureah/Miriah/Uriah (Lidyard) Marks.[40] She was born about 1745 probably in Pennsylvania and died 1 April 1817 in Loudoun County, Virginia.[41]

---

[37] DAR application of Leona (Dewey) Cryer, #677790, 12257 Shafton Road, Spring Hill, FL 34608, 23 August 1983.

[38] Hugh and Margaret Howell, parents of William, were in Hunterdon County, NJ from the early 1700s to about 1763. (Roxanne K. Carkhuff, Hunterdon Genealogical Services, to Richard Wallace, 15 April 1991).

[39] DAR application of Barbara White Herring, #655704, 4549 Mono Drive, Toledo, OH 43623, 18 March 1981.

[40] J. Estelle Stewart King, Abstracts of Wills, Inventories, and Administration Accounts of Loudoun County, Virginia, 1757-1800 (Baltimore: Genealogical Publishing, 1984), p. 35.

[41] DAR application of Mary Irvin Newman, #418825, 5115 Fairglen Lane, Chevy Chase, MD, 17 August 1953.

One of the earliest records for William in Loudoun County was his appearance on the list of tithables in 1771 in Shelburne Parish.[42] Living near him were his father, Hugh, and brothers Andrew, Abner, John, and Benjamin.   William was a Revolutionary War soldier, having served under Captain Henry McCabe as a sergeant.[43] At least one descendant of William Howell claims, through family tradition, that William Howell was a Quaker, but was read out of the faith because he married out of the Meeting and for engaging in military activity.[44]   William was named executor of his father's will, which was written 6 March 1777 and probated the following 12 May.[45] William's name appears on the Loudoun County land tax records for 1782.[46]   He was taxed on 125 acres, probably the land that was left his mother during her lifetime. He was taxed on the same acreage for the years 1783-1786.[47]

William shows up in personal property tax lists for 1787-1791, 1793, 1795 and 1799.[48] In 1788, his son Jesse is listed in his household. In 1793, Abel Howell is listed in his household. In 1799, Abner Howell is similarly listed. For some of these tax lists, additional males in a household, age 16-21 were listed. Sometimes all males

---

[42] Pollyanna Creekmore, "Loudoun County, Virginia 1771 Tithable List," v. 16, p. 243, v. 17, p. 11.

[43] Louis A. Burgess, comp., Virginia Soldiers of 1776 (Richmond, VA: Richmond Press, 1929), p. 1267.

[44] Estelle Howell Smith to Mrs. Kenneth Troy Trewhella, Registrar General, N.S.D.A.R., Washington, D.C., 6 April 1953. Copies in possession of authors.

[45] J. Estelle Stewart King, Abstracts, p. 13.

[46] Loudoun County Land Tax Records (1782), Microfilm #1, filmed by Virginia State Library, Richmond, VA, N. pag., Copy available at Thomas Balch Library, Leesburg, VA.

[47] Ibid., (1783-1786), N. pag.

[48] Loudoun County Personal Property Tax List, (1787-1791, 1793, 1795, 1799), Part 2: 1787-1797; Part 3: 1798-1812, N. pag.

over age 16 were included. William received payment when his brother-in-law's, Capt. Isaiah Marks, estate was settled 10 September 1791.[49] There is record of his leasing land from Thomas Humphrey on 11 June 1810.[50] William died, intestate, 4 April 1817. The estate settlement, which was handled by his oldest son, Jesse, showed that son, Abner, had been paid "for keeping his father & mother."[51] It was not uncommon for aging parents to live with one of their children.

William's father-in-law, the Reverend John Marks, has been the subject of an active group of researchers.[52] According to their work, John Marks was first found in public records in Montgomery County, Pennsylvania, when he was baptized (Baptist) on 10 August 1740 at the age of 24. They place his ordination as a Baptist minister at about 1748. John and Uriah Marks were dismissed from the Montgomery Baptist Church 12 August 1761 to go to Virginia. In Virginia, the Reverend Marks took up the Ministry at Ketoctin Baptist Church in Loudoun County, where he served until 1785. The records of the Philadelphia Baptist Association reveal that the Ketoctin Church was constituted in 1751 and was received into the Association in 1754.[53] It is the oldest existing church of the Baptist denomination in Virginia.[54] The church and its adjoining cemetery, where John Marks is buried, occupy a nearly 11 acre tract fronting on State Routes 711 and 716 about two miles north of route 7 in Loudoun County. Both the creek which runs through the property and the

---

[49] Loudoun County, VA, Will Bk D:200.

[50] Loudoun County, VA, Deed Bk 2L:354.

[51] Loudoun County, VA, Will Bk M:304.

[52] Our information came from Frances Jones, 108 St. Leo Drive, Cahokia, IL 62206.

[53] William Vernon Ford, ed., Ketoctin Chronicle (Leesburg, VA: Potomac Press, 1965), pp. 3-4.

[54] Robert Baylor Semple, History of the Baptists in Virginia (Cottonport, LA: Polyanthos, 1972), p. 394.

hes at this location have been known by the Indian , translated to mean "the ancient wooded hill." ᴛᴀdιtιon tells us two log structures were replaced by a stone building, which in turn was replaced by the current red brick church in 1854.[55] During the Revolution, Rev. Marks was an ardent speaker against the British. According to one source, "So intense did the patriotic sentiment become under the festering zeal of Marks that nearly every man of military age in that section enlisted in the American army. Two of his sons, Isaiah and John, as well as a son-in-law, William Howell, enlisted in Morgan's Riflemen, and Isaiah was soon promoted to captain."[56] Marks died in 1788. His will, which was filed for probate 4 April 1788 lists "Martha Howell (hus. William)" as one of his heirs.[57]

Known children of William and Martha (Marks) Howell include:[58]

+11   i.   Jesse[3] Howell, born 9 February 1770/71, Shelburne Parish, Loudoun County, Virginia.

+12   ii.   Abner Howell, born 27 August 1775, Virginia.

+13   iii.   Abel Howell, born 28 December 1778, Virginia

+14   iv.   Margaret Howell, born 2 September 1782, Virginia.

---

[55] Ford, Ketoctin Chronicle, p. 33.

[56] J.V. Nichols, "The Rev. John Marks Roused the Loudoun Countryside to Warfare Against British," The Blue Ridge Herald (Purcellville, Loudoun Co., VA), 15 July 1954, pp. 9, 16. Nichols was a great great grandson of William Howell.

[57] J. Estelle Stewart King, Abstracts, p. 35.

[58] DAR application of Jessie C. Tomlinsen, #528853, 3626 Alabama Ave., Washington, D.C., 8 April 1967.

3. Andrew[2] Howell (Hugh[1]) was another son listed in Hugh Howell's will.[59]   We have few facts about him and many unanswered questions, including when he died, who he married, and the names of his children. As explained below, we do have a pretty good idea when and where he was born.

Andrew is mentioned for the first time in the 1769 Loudoun County Tithable List.[60] He was 16 years or older at the time, and was living in the household of Hugh Howell. He was not listed for 1768 or earlier years when his father was listed. This absence suggests that Andrew attained age 16 in 1769, and was probably born in 1753. Birth in that year means he was born in New Jersey where his family lived at the time.

Andrew was again listed in Hugh's household in 1771.[61]   Also included in the household were brothers Benjamin and John.

Andrew was taxed in Loudoun County in 1782 based on his ownership of three horses and five cattle.[62] The next year he was taxed on the same livestock.[63] Neighbors also taxed in 1783 were brothers Benjamin, William, and mother, "Margrate."

The year 1783 is significant for Andrew as far as genealogical research is concerned. This is the last year he appears in Loudoun County tax records. His relatives continue to be taxed in Loudoun County for a number of years to come. What happened to him? We really don't know for sure.

---

[59] Loudoun County, VA, Will Bk B:176.

[60] Sparacio, eds., Tithables Loudoun County, Virginia: 1758-1769, p. 87.

[61] Pollyanna Creekmore, "Loudoun County, Virginia 1771 Tithable List," v. 17, p. 11.

[62] Loudoun County Personal Property Tax List (1782), Part 1: 1782-1787, Battalion 1, N. pag.

[63] Ibid., (1783).

Andrew died about 1783. If he did, he did not leave a will, ana a probate record for his estate is not recorded in Loudoun County. It's interesting to note here that Andrew's name is not mentioned in his father's 1804 estate accounting.[64] In fact the only children mentioned in this document were Reuben, William, Abner, Benjamin, and Rachel. However, if Andrew left the state in the 1780's and had no further contact with his family, he would not be found in the estate accounting.

If Andrew left Virginia, his destination may have been either Hardin County, Kentucky or Monroe County, Ohio. Both of these counties are on the Ohio River, which was the migration route used by many settlers of that era.

An Andrew Howell cannot be found in the 1790 Kentucky Census, but there was one in the 1800 Kentucky Census. This Andrew was living in Hardin County.[65] Living in the same county in 1800 were Charles Howel, John Howel, John Howel Jr., and Jacob Howel.

An Andrew Howell was not found in the 1810 Kentucky Census Index. An Andrew Howell left an 1818 Hardin County will.[66] This county could be an area for further research.

Another area for research could be Monroe County, Ohio. The 1820 Census lists no fewer than three Andrew Howells in that county. The two living in Salem Township were 45 years or older.[67]

---

[64] Loudoun County, VA, Will Bk G:217.

[65] Glenn Clift, Second Census of Kentucky 1800 (Baltimore: Genealogical Publishing Co., 1970), p. 142.

[66] Ronald V. Jackson, ed. Index to Kentucky Wills to 1851 (Provo, UT: Accelerated Indexing, 1979), p. 41.

[67] 1820 federal census, population schedule, Salem Township, Monroe County, OH, p. 121.

The other Andrew was a younger man (16-26), who was living in Ohio Township.[68] Monroe County is directly below Belmont County where we know other Loudoun County Howells lived.

As readers can see, Andrew is an unfinished product. There is still much to be learned about him. We can speculate that he moved to either Kentucky or Ohio, but we really don't know for sure what happened to him after 1783.

4. John[2] Howell (Hugh) was also named in the Hugh Howell will.[69] He was listed for the first time in his father's Loudoun County household in the 1769 Tithable List.[70] This means he was born on or before 1753, probably in New Jersey where his family lived at the time. Other vital information on him is lacking.

Hugh's son John was not the only John Howell in Loudoun County during the last half of the 18th century. There were at least two other John Howells, possibly relatives, taxed in Loudoun County as early as 1762.[71] A Hezekiah Howell was living in the household of one of these John Howells. Either one or both of these Johns continued to be taxed in Loudoun County throughout the 1760s.

John was still living with his father in 1771.[72] Also living in Hugh's household were brothers Andrew and Benjamin. A John Howell served in the Revolutionary War, but we can't say for certain that this John was Hugh's son. His service record shows that he enlisted for

---

[68] Ibid., p. 122.

[69] Loudoun County, VA, Will Bk B:176.

[70] Sparacio, eds., Tithables Loudoun County, Virginia: 1758-1769, p. 87.

[71] Ibid., pp. 17, 18.

[72] Pollyanna Creekmore, "Loudoun County Virginia 1771 Tithable List," v. 17, p. 11.

a period of one year.[73] He served as a private in the ninth Virginia Regiment in Captain Robert Beall's Company. His Colonel was John Gibson.   This unit was originally designated the 13th Virginia Regiment.

The service record consists of three muster rolls dated April, June, and October 1779, which show that John was stationed at Ft. Pitt (Pittsburgh, Pennsylvania) from October 1778 to 9 August 1779, his discharge date.

A book of Loudoun County records contains a section titled <u>Families of Soldiers in the Continental Army Ordered Provided for on the date given</u>.[74] In the list of families is the name "Howell, John, wife, 9 February 1779." As previously stated, we really don't know for sure if these war records refer to Hugh's son. There were several men named John Howell in Loudoun County, not to mention other counties in Virginia and Pennsylvania.

A John Howell continues to be taxed in Loudoun County in the 1780s and 1790s. For 1782 and 1785, he was taxed in Battalion 1.[75] From 1787-1795, a John Howell was taxed in Battalion 2.[76] In 1789, a John Howell, Jr. was living in his household. In 1795 Jr. is still living with him, as well as a "Landin" Howell.

---

[73] Compiled Service Records of Soldiers Who Served in the American Army During the Revolutionary War, National Archives and Records Service, Washington, D.C., 1976, Microfilm M881, Roll 1058.

[74] J. Estelle Stewart King, <u>Abstracts</u>, p. 57.

[75] Loudoun County Personal Property Tax List, (1782, 1785), Part 1: 1782-1787, Battalion 1, N. pag.

[76] Ibid., (1787, 1788, 1789, 1795), Part 1: 1782-1787; Part 2: 1787-1797, Battalion 2, N. pag.

We don't know if Hugh's son survived much beyond 1777. He is not mentioned in his father's 1804 estate accounting.[77] We don't know whom he married or the names of his children. Research on him is complicated by the fact that many John Howells can be found in Virginia, Pennsylvania, Kentucky and Ohio. Perhaps with time, more will be learned about him.

5. Abner[2] Howell (Hugh[1]) was another son named in Hugh Howell's 1777 will.[78] Beyond that fact, there are many questions about this son to be resolved. Abner must be standing at the edge of the universe, laughing at the seemingly puny research efforts of his 20th century descendants. This research does tend to point to the existence of several Abner Howells, who lived in Virginia and Pennsylvania. Which one belongs to Hugh Howell is a matter for conjecture and further research. The evidence does suggest that our Abner was born in New Jersey before 1755. All other vital data for him is inconclusive. The pieces of this interesting and frustrating puzzle will be presented in the following paragraphs.

The first Virginia record found for an Abner Howell is the 1762 Tithable List for Loudoun County. The listing shows a Daniel and an Abner Howell living in the household of Timothy Howell.[79] This listing is interesting in that Abner is not included in the household of Hugh Howell, who was also listed that year with son, William.[80] Timothy could very well be related to Hugh, but this has not been established. The record suggests that this Abner is Timothy's son. Tithables included males over 16 years old, so this Abner was born on or before 1746.

---

[77] Loudoun County, VA, Will Bk G:217.

[78] Loudoun County, VA, Will Bk B:176.

[79] Sparacio, eds. <u>Tithables Loudoun County, Virginia: 1758-1769</u>, p. 17.

[80] Ibid., p. 18.

The estate accounting of Richard Roberts prepared 8 November 1763 and recorded 15 February 1764, refers to estate debts paid to various people, including an Abner Howell.[81]

After an absence from the record for three years, Abner shows up in the 1765 Tithable List. Again he is listed in the household of Timothy Howell.[82] In 1767, Abner is in a separate household, listed directly below Timothy Howell.[83]

An Abner shows up for the first time in Hugh Howell's household in the 1768 listing.[84] This Abner would have been born before 1752. Only one Abner appears in the 1768 listing.

The 1769 listing gives us two Abners to consider. One is in the household of George Gregg, along with an Elisha Gregg and a Hugh Owens.[85] The other is a head of household that includes a David Howell and Thomas Howell.[86]

This is a good time to mention an interesting Quaker record found by the authors. This record is part of the minutes of the Fairfax Monthly Meeting, Virginia. The record refers to a Mary Gregg (now Howel), who married out of unity 30 December 1769, moved far away, and was disowned.[87] The Greggs were a well documented Quaker family from Chester County, Pennsylvania. The record does not identify Mary's husband's first name, but it is interesting to speculate that it

[81] Loudoun County, VA, Will Bk A:99-101.

[82] Sparacio, eds., Tithables Loudoun County, Virginia: 1758-1769, p. 35.

[83] Ibid., p. 45.

[84] Ibid., p. 59.

[85] Ibid., p. 82.

[86] Ibid., p. 88.

[87] William W. Hinshaw, Encyclopedia of America Quaker Genealogy (Baltimore, MD: Genealogical Publishing, 1973), p. 497.

might have been the Abner Howell we found in the 1769 household of George Gregg. As readers will soon learn, family tradition tells us an Abner Howell married a Gregg, not Mary but Nancy.

The same minutes refer to a Lydia Gregg (now Howell) who married outside meeting 27 September 1777.[88] She was disowned that same day. We know she married Benjamin Howell, Abner's brother. More will be written about her in Benjamin's section.

In the 1771 Tithable List, again only one Abner Howell shows up. This time he is a head of household that included an Archibald McNail.[89] Timothy Howell also puts in his customary appearance. A Thomas and David Howell are living in his household.[90] These could very well be the two men who were in Abner's household in 1769.

In December 1770, an Abner Howell, along with George Gregg and Owen Roberts witnessed the will of Thomas John.[91] Witnesses to an important event like this were often related either to each other, the heirs or to the will maker. Research to date has not proved any such relationships, but for future reference Thomas John named as heirs his daughters Rachel Reynolds, Jane Cox (of Carolina), Susannah Matthews (of Maryland), and Mary Harris (wife of Samuel Harris. Named executor was Richard Williams.

The year 1774 is the last year in which we find an older generation Abner Howell in Loudoun County tax records.[92] This statement is also intended to cover personal property tax records from 1782

---

[88] Ibid., p. 497.

[89] Pollyanna Creekmore, "Loudoun County, Virginia 1771 Tithable List," v. 16, p. 244.

[90] Ibid.

[91] J. Estelle Stewart King, Abstracts, p. 8.

[92] Sparacio, eds. Tithables of Loudoun County, Virginia: 1770-1774, p. 82.

through 1795. He/they either left Loudoun County or died. If death did occur in Loudoun County, the Abners we have found did not leave an estate there. This name does not appear in Loudoun County estate records for applicable periods.

The name Abner Howell shows up in Loudoun County land records, too. When Matthew Hickson (Hixon) bought 464 acres of land along Catoctin Creek 18 May 1764, the transaction was signed in the presence of Timothy Howell, John Howell and Abner Howell.[93] The previous day he was present when Hugh Howell bought his 125 acres that partly bordered the Hixon property. Also present were Timothy Howell and John Howell.

On 17 November 1770, an Abner Howell bought for "£100 current money," 150 acres of land from John Compton.[94] Said Compton signed the deed in the presence of Thomas Amos, William (his mark) Hurley and Timothy Howell. A margin note to this deed dated 31 August 1773 shows that this property was examined and deeded to Timothy Howell.

A transaction dated 6 April 1775 between Bryan Fairfax of Fairfax County, Warner Washington of Frederick County and William Janney of Loudoun County was witnessed by Abner Howell and Timothy Howell.[95] Timothy proved the transaction 15 August 1775.

Where did the two Abners go, if still alive, after the 1760's and 1770's? One may have gone to Botetourt County, Virginia. An Abner Howell is found there on the tax list for 1784.[96] In fact no

---

[93] Ibid., p. 52-53.

[94] Loudoun County, VA, Deed Bk H:224.

[95] Sparacio, eds. Deed Abstracts of Loudoun County, Virginia: 1775-1778, pp. 3-4.

[96] Augusta B. Fothergill, Virginia Taxpayers 1782-87 (Baltimore: Genealogical Publishing, 1986), p. 63.

fewer than eight Howells were there. The name is spelled Howel in this alphabetical record, for the most part.

Abner Howel	Donald Howel
Benjamin Howel	John Howel
Charles Howel	Joshuae Howel
David Howel	Thomas Howell

On 12 September 1786, Abner Howell bought 1070 acres of land in Botetourt County from a John Mills, Jr. and Mary McIntire, the widow of John Mills, Sr.[97] This land was situated on Wolf Creek and Falling Creek, branches of the Roanoke River. The purchase price was "£1000 current money." If this is the Abner Howell who bought land in Loudoun County, he had come a long way since paying £100 for 150 acres of land in 1770. However, the history of America is full of stories like this.

By their deed dated 11 August 1802, Daniel James and Thomas Bandy granted to Mathew Pate, Charles Horn, Abner Howell, Stephen Ferril, Samuel James, and James Howell, Trustees of the Blueridge Meeting House, a tract of land near the county line, containing 2 acres and 64 poles, upon which to build a meeting house and for use as a burial ground.[98] Less than two years later, the Strawberry Association of the Baptist Church met there, suggesting that the membership must have been composed mostly of Baptists.[99]

Records found in the basement of the courthouse in Fincastle, Virginia, reveal that the Botetourt County Abner Howell had military service during the Revolutionary War. The record dated 31 August

---

[97] Botetourt County, VA, Deed Bk 3:419.

[98] Botetourt County, VA, Deed Bk 8:38.

[99] Robert D. Stoner, <u>A Seedbed of the Republic</u> (Kingsport, TN: Kingsport Press, 1962), p. 125.

1782 shows the county's quota of troops as of that date.[100]
Recorded along with Abner Howell were Danl Howell, "Danile"
Howell, John Howell, and a Danl Hickson.

This Abner Howell died about 1812 based on his will dated October
1812.[101] In this document, which he signed in longhand, he names
his wife Hannah and children James, Samuel, Thomas, Jesse, David,
Jemima Rader, Mary Gish and Ruth Gish. Named executors were
sons James, Samuel and Jesse.

If readers are not already baffled enough by the Howell names found
in Botetourt County, many of which bear much similarity to some
found in Loudoun County, let's add to the equation the Howells found
in Bedford County, Virginia in the 1810 census.[102] Besides a 45+
year old Abner Howell, there is a 45+ year old Thomas. In the 26-44
year old category are two Davids, a Jesse, a John, a Samuel, a Thomas
and a William. Bedford County borders Botetourt County, so it's
possible that some of the first Abner's children could be found there.
However, this does not explain the finding of the second Abner there.
The first Abner was enumerated as expected in Botetourt County as
a 45+ year old "Abnor" Howell.[103]

More research will be needed to unravel these tangled Howell threads
in Virginia. Perhaps publication of what is known so far will
stimulate more research by other interested parties.

A review of the 1820 federal census index for Virginia does not reveal
any Abner Howells that year. This absence suggests that the

---

[100] Anna L. Worrell, comp., Early Marriages, Wills, & Some Revolutionary War
Records, Botetourt County, Virginia (Baltimore, MD: Genealogical Publishing,
1975), pp. 66-69.

[101] Botetourt County, VA, Will Bk B:304.

[102] R.V. Jackson & G.R. Teeples, eds., Virginia 1810 Census Index (Bountiful,
UT: Accelerated Indexing, 1978), p. 158.

[103] Ibid, p. 158.

remaining Abner Howell in Bedford County either died or left the state.

There is one more record that should be discussed before we leave Virginia for Pennsylvania. This record details the military service of a Private Abner Howell who enlisted 6 September 1777 for a period of three years.[104] He served in the 10th Virginia Regiment, the merged 1st and 10th Virginia Regiment and the 14th Virginia Regiment. Most of the nearly 50 muster and payroll records for Private Howell date from 1778 and 1779. While in the service, this Abner was paid 6 2/3 dollars a month. His Company Captain during the majority of this period was Peter Jones. The Colonel was usually either Charles Lewis or William Davies.

The places where Abner was stationed during the war included Valley Forge, Pennsylvania (March - May 1778), Brunswick, Pennsylvania (?) (June 1778), White Plains, New York (July - August 1778), West Point, New York (September 1778), Fish Kill, New York (October - December 1778), and Middle Brook, New York (?) (January - April 1779). The records from Fish Kill reveal that he was ill during those three months.

Revolutionary War records of this type do not reveal any personal information about the soldier, such as date of birth, address, parents' names, etc. We can't say with any certainty that the soldier was Hugh's son. The proof simply is not there. A search of pension and bounty land claims at the National Archives Branch in Kansas City established that this Abner Howell did not file for those benefits.

Another candidate for Hugh Howell's son is the Abner Howell who lived in Washington County, Pennsylvania in the early 1780's. The present day eastern border of this western Pennsylvania county is the Monongahela River, one of the migration routes other Howells used when they moved to Ohio in the early 1800's.

---

[104] Compiled Service Records of Soldiers Who Served in American Army During the Revolutionary War, National Archives & Trust Fund Board, Washington, 1976; National Archives Microfilm M881, Role 924.

When the Effective Supply Tax for Washington County was recorded in 1781, an Abner Howel was taxed on 200 acres, 2 horses and 2 sheep in Amwell Township.[105] It could be coincidental, but there is an Amwell Township in Hunterdon County, New Jersey. Part of this township abuts Hopewell Township (formerly in Hunterdon County, now in Mercer County, New Jersey) where Hugh Howell lived at one time. In the same township lived a single man by the name of Daniel Howell. He was taxed on 100 acres and one horse.[106]

Other Howells in Washington County lived in Donegal Township. These four men, John, Aaron (single), Thomas (single), and John Howel, did not own land, but were taxed on their ownership of livestock.[107]

This Abner Howell, like the other Abners we've encountered, served in the military during the American Revolution. He was a Captain in the Washington County Militia.[108] Privates in his company were John Howel, John Howell, Jr., Jacob Howell, and Jonathan Howell.

Another listing of soldiers in the Revolution includes the names of Abner Howell, Captain, and Privates Daniel, Jacob, John, and Thomas

[105] William Henry Egle, ed. Pennsylvania Archives (Third Series) 22 (Harrisburg: Wm. Stanley Ray, State Printer, 1897), p. 703.

[106] Ibid., p. 705.

[107] John B. Linn & Wm. H. Egle, eds., Pennsylvania Archives (Third Series), 4 (Harrisburg, PA: E.K. Myers, State Printer, 1890), p. 741.

[108] Thomas L. Montgomery, ed., Pennsylvania Archives (Fifth Series) 4 (Harrisburg, PA: State Printer, 1906) p. 712.

Howell.[109]   Those receiving depreciation pay during the period 1783-1788 for service in the Washington County Militia were Captain Abner Howell and privates Daniel, Jacob, John (2) and Jonathan.[110]

Abner Howell also served as a Washington County Justice of the Peace in Amwell District. The date of his appointment was 15 July 1781.[111]

Land surveys taken in Washington County, Pennsylvania from 1784-1892 show that Abner Howell's 300 acres were surveyed 26 September 1785.[112]

The Washington County Abner disappears from Pennsylvania after 1785. He is not found in either the 1790 or 1800 federal census for Pennsylvania. There is good evidence that he left the state for Kentucky. We still find a Daniel Howell and a Jonathan Howell in Washington County in 1790.[113]

At this point, we should mention a family tradition that the authors have heard from several other researchers. The story varies in some details, but the basic elements remain the same. Tradition states that Abner Howell married a Nancy Gregg, served in the American Revolution, and eventually moved to Kentucky, where he died in Bracken County either in 1794 or 1797. We have been able to verify much of this story. We did find an Abner Howell in the late 1760s in the Loudoun County family of George Gregg. We also know that several Abners had military service during the American Revolution,

[109] Ibid.

[110] Ibid., p. 404.

[111] Boyd Crumrine, ed., History of Washington County, Pennsylvania (Philadelphia: L.H. Everts & Co., 1882), p. 652.

[112] Wm. H. Egle, ed., Pennsylvania Archives (Third Series) v. 26, p. 565.

[113] Ronald Vern Jackson, ed., 1790 Federal Census of Pennsylvania (Bountiful, UT: Accelerated Indexing Systems, 1978), pp. 255, 257 .

but which one, if any of them, is the son of Hugh Howell? That's the problem.

Adding to the family tradition story, an Abner Howell is mentioned in a genealogical book that details the pioneer families of Hopewell, New Jersey. According to this book, Job Stout, son of Jonathan, married Rhoda, daughter of Abner Howell.[114] Job Stout moved to Mays Lick (now Maysville), Kentucky 1788-1790. Maysville is in Mason County. Part of Mason County became Bracken County in 1797.

In another part of his book, Mr. Ege mentions that Rhoda Howell was born 3 May 1771, the daughter of Abner and Mary Howell.[115] They were supposedly a Quaker family living in Bucks County, Pennsylvania, near Trenton, New Jersey. Rhoda reportedly married Job Stout in 1786.

Ralph Ege does not list sources in his book, but his story is mostly verified by the Revolutionary War Pension file of Job Stout.[116] This file contains an 1832 military service affidavit by Job Stout, with character statements from William Tyner and Joab Howell; an 1844 affidavit by Rhoda Stout that she is the widow of Job; an 1844 affidavit by Joab Howell that he attended the wedding celebration of his sister, Rhoda, in 1787 when he was 9 years old; pages from a family Bible that establish the birth dates of Rhoda Howell, Job Stout, and their 13 children.

The pension file establishes the following facts. Job Stout was born 21 February 1763, at Hopewell, New Jersey. He first entered military service in 1779 at Greenwich Township, Sussex County, New Jersey. In 1780, he moved to Northampton County, Pennsylvania. On 7

[114] Ralph Ege, <u>Pioneers of Old Hopewell</u> (Hopewell, NJ: reprinted by the Hopewell Museum, 1965), pp. 93-94.

[115] Ibid., p. 282.

[116] Revolutionary War Pension File of Job Stout (W9668), National Archives Microfilm M804, Roll 2309.

August 1787, he married Rhoda Howell in Washington County, Pennsylvania. She was born when Ralph Ege said she was. Job died 28 February 1833, probably in Franklin County, Indiana. Rhoda died 12 April 1847, also probably in Franklin County, Indiana. The pension due Job Stout and his widow, Rhoda, was allowed December 1850. The monies due were paid to their surviving children, namely Mary Shirk, Rachel Cummins, Abner Stout, Elizabeth Shirk, Joab Stout, David Stout, Sarah Holliday, Ira Stout, Aaron Stout, and Rebecca Goudie. Jonathan, Anna and Margaret pre-deceased their parents.

In addition to the excellent evidence in the pension file, the second census of Kentucky shows a Jobe Stout and a Mary Howell living in Bracken County.[117] In adjacent Mason County, we find Jonathan Stout, David Stout, and an Abraham Stout.[118] An Abner Howell died intestate in Bracken County. His 1797 inventory contains no family data.[119]

This section has summarized the research that has been conducted to find out more about Abner Howell, a person who has proved to be quite elusive. We still do not know which of the Abners we have found outside of Loudoun County connects directly to Hugh Howell. Perhaps none of them do. It's also possible that Hugh's son died as a young man in his 20's. If that is true, we will probably not be able to prove it unless a family Bible record miraculously appears. Such records are quite rare for the 18th century.

Interesting points to ponder are two entries on Hugh Howell's 1804 estate accounting. The accounting, consisting of roughly 40 entries, lists "cash -Abner Howell proved acct - £5," and "cash - Will. Howell part of Abners Estate - £1."[120] Do these entries mean Abner died

---

[117] Glenn Clift, <u>Second Census of Kentucky 1800</u>, pp. 284, 143.

[118] Ibid., p. 284.

[119] Bracken County, KY, Will Bk A:6-8.

[120] Loudoun County, VA, Will Bk G:217.

prior to the final accounting? The other heirs are all listed by name and then the cash amount they received. Abner is the only one handled differently.

It's pretty clear that the Abner Howell in Washington County, Pennsylvania is not the same Abner who lived in Botetourt County, Virginia. One was still living in Pennsylvania in 1785, while the other was being taxed the previous year in Virginia.

It's interesting to speculate that Timothy Howell was the father of one of the Abners we found in Loudoun County. However, Timothy's 1794 will does not list Abner as an heir.[121] The will refers to sons Samuel, Mahlon, and Thomas. Incidentally this will has a Quaker style date (5th day of 2nd month 1794). Timothy and his wife, Rebecca, have been found in Virginia Quaker records, but Abner was not found there. If Abner died young without heirs, he would not have been mentioned in his father's will.

Finally, we don't know for sure if Abner Howell ever married or whom he married. The Botetourt Abner married a woman named Hannah, but we don't know her maiden name or when they married. The Washington County Abner probably married a woman named Mary. The evidence suggests her maiden name could have been Gregg. This family moved to Kentucky where Abner died in the 1790s.

The same goes for Abner's children. We don't know their names, or even if he had any for that matter. The Abners we've found had children, but this brings us back to our original question. Which Abner is the right Abner? We end this section with the plea: "Will the correct Abner Howell please stand up?"

---

[121] Loudoun County, VA, Will Bk E:22.

6. Benjamin[2] Howell (Hugh[1]) was born about 1755[122] probably in New Jersey,[123] and died 1830 in Flushing, Belmont County, Ohio.[124] He married Lydia Gregg, daughter of John and Susannah (Curle) Gregg, in 1777 in Loudoun County, Virginia. She was born 2 August 1756 in Chester County, Pennsylvania and died 1844 in Flushing.[125] A Gregg genealogy also states that she was born 12 August 1756 and died in Ohio and married a Howell.[126] From Johnson we learn that:

> John Howell emigrated from Loudoun County, Virginia, to Belmont County, Ohio about 1805 to about one half mile south of Flushing. He returned to Virginia in 1806 to bring his father, Benjamin Howell, *b. c. 1755* and the rest of the family floating down the Monongahela and Ohio Rivers on a flatboat, landing opposite Wheeling, West Virginia, and going westward to a cabin prepared for them. He took up quarter sections of land directly from government grant, signed by James Madison, President, and James Monroe, Secretary of State in 1811 and 1812. His house was built in 1815 and still standing in 1902.[127]

---

[122] T. Lester Johnson, The Howell Family History, rev. (Akron, OH: author, 1979), p. 2. Johnson resided at 1040 Victoria Drive, Bucyrus, OH 44820 in 1993.

[123] See section on Hugh Howell for speculation on place of birth.

[124] Johnson, The Howell Family History, p. 2.

[125] Ibid., p. 2. Also Loudoun County, VA, Will Bk C:338-341 (will of John Gregg witnessed 2 December 1787).

[126] Hazel May Middleton Kendall, Quaker Greggs (Anderson, IN: 1944; reprinted Jenner, CA: Richard T. & Newton K. Gregg, 1979), p. 211.

[127] Johnson, The Howell Family History, **p. 2.**

Most of the information in this quotation was a paraphrase of a description by Caldwell.[128]

Children of Benjamin and Lydia include:[129]

15	i.	Daniel[3] Howell, born 1777 in Virginia.
16	ii.	Margaret Howell, born 1780 in Virginia.
+17	iii.	John Howell, born 13 January 1784 in Loudoun County, Virginia.[130] *"Capt"* ?
18	iv.	Jonathan Howell, born 1786 in Virginia.
19	v.	Sarah Howell, born 1788.
20	vi.	Ann Howell, born 1790.
21	vii.	William Howell, born 1792 in Virginia.
22	viii.	Rachel Howell, born 1796 in Virginia.
23	ix.	Elizabeth Howell, born 1798.

7.   Daniel[2] Howell (Hugh[1]) was listed as an heir in his father's will.[131]   Much like his brothers, Abner, John and Andrew, we know

---

[128] J.A. Caldwell, <u>History of Belmont and Jefferson Counties, Ohio</u> (Wheeling WV: Historical Publishing, 1880), p. 380.

[129] Johnson, <u>The Howell Family History</u>, p. 2.

[130] Caldwell, <u>History of Belmont and Jefferson Counties</u>, p. 380; also <u>Biographical Record Harrison, Ohio</u> (Chicago: J.H. Beers & Co., 1891), pp. 183-184.

[131] Loudoun County, VA, Will Bk B:176.

very little about him. Hugh's son was probably born about 1757 in New Jersey, but he was not the only Daniel Howell in Loudoun County.

The first record of a Daniel Howell in Loudoun County, Virginia was the 1762 Tithable List.[132] This Daniel Howell was recorded in the household of Timothy Howell, and would have been born on or before 1746.

A Daniel Howell shows up as a head of household in Loudoun County for the years 1767-1769.[133]

Land records reveal that in 1770, a Daniel Howell, Sr. and his wife, Elizabeth, deeded 455 acres of land in Cameron Parish to a Daniel Howell, Jr.[134] This property is in northwest Loudoun County - north of Hillsboro and west of Short Hills. The transaction was completed in the presence of John Howell. These Daniels, probably father and son, could very well be related to Hugh Howell in some way, but a direct relationship is unlikely. The deeding of land suggests that Daniel, Jr. was of legal age, which means that he was born by 1749 or earlier. Daniel, Sr. would also have been age 21 or older when Jr. was born. He may have been older, but he would have been born by 1728 at the latest.

A Daniel Howell continues to appear in Loudoun County tax records, e.g., 1771 and 1782.[135] Each time he is listed as a head of household. The one listed in 1782 owned 4 slaves, 2 horses, and 8 cattle. The tax record for 1782 is the last record we found for him in Loudoun County. If he died about that year, he did not leave an

---

[132] Sparacio, eds., <u>Tithables Loudoun County, Virginia 1758-1769</u>, p. 17.

[133] Ibid., pp. 45, 59, 83.

[134] Loudoun County, VA, Deed Bk H.

[135] Pollyanna Creekmore, "Loudoun County, Virginia 1771 Tithable List," <u>Virginia Genealogist</u> 16 (Oct.-Dec. 1972):244. Loudoun County Personal Property Tax List (1782), Part 1: 1782-1787, Battalion 1, N. pag.

estate that was probated in Loudoun County. These records were
checked and his name was not found.

A Daniel Howell served in the Revolutionary War, and some
researchers have said this Daniel was Hugh's son. Soldiers of the
Revolution are always popular when it comes to assigning heirs to a
particular ancestor. However, a review of this Daniel Howell's
pension file makes him an unlikely heir of Hugh Howell.

On his pension application dated 21 September 1832, which was filed
in Floyd County, Virginia, this Daniel Howell stated that he was born
in 1759 in Philadelphia County, Pennsylvania.[136] At the time of his
enlistment in 1776, he was residing in Botetourt County, Virginia. He
had at least three periods of service from 1776 to 1781 as a private.
His file shows that he was awarded a pension of $30 a year and that
he died 6 March 1836. He left a widow named Frances.

Private Daniel Howell was born in 1759, which would make him
eligible to be Hugh Howell's son. The fact that this birth took place
in Philadelphia County, Pennsylvania puts their relationship in the
doubtful category. As far as we know, Hugh was still living in
Hunterdon County, New Jersey when this Daniel was born. Also, a
17-year old boy (probable age at enlistment) would have been living
with his family in Loudoun County, not in a county many miles from
home.

The Daniels we've been writing about were most likely not Hugh's
son. His son first appears as a tithable in his family in the year 1773,
meaning he was born about 1757.[137] He appears again in his
father's household in 1774.[138] His brother Benjamin was also listed
in his father's family as a tithable for both years. We don't know if

---

[136] Revolutionary War Pension File for Daniel Howell (S13413), National
Archives Microfilm M804, Roll 1346.

[137] Sparacio, eds., Tithables Loudoun County, Virginia: 1770-1774, p. 64.

[138] Ibid., p. 79.

Daniel survived to marry or have children. A number of Daniel Howells have been found in Virginia, Kentucky, Pennsylvania and Ohio, but we can't be sure if any of them properly belong to Hugh Howell. Next to John, Daniel is probably the most popular given name among Howells of that era. This makes the work of a genealogist that much harder.

8. Reuben[2] Howell (Hugh[1]) was born 26 February 1762 near Trenton, New Jersey. He probably died before 1840 in Ohio. Vital information on his wife has not been found. This record of birth along with valuable information on the Howell family move from New Jersey to Loudoun County was discovered in his pension file.[139] When he filed in 1832, he gave testimony before a Court convened in Columbiana County, Ohio. At the age of 15 months, his father moved to Loudoun County, state of Virginia. When Reuben entered the service in 1780 he was still living in Loudoun County. He went on to say that after the war he lived in Loudoun County until 1810 when he moved to Columbiana County, Ohio. At the time he filed his application, he was living in Salem Township of the same county.

Reuben was the seventh of seven sons born to Hugh and Margaret Howell. He was listed as an heir in his father's 1777 will.[140] When his father's estate was finally settled in 1804, Reuben Howell was mentioned by name in those documents.[141]

Either at the end of August or 1 September 1780, Reuben volunteered for military service in the Revolutionary War.[142] His first enlistment lasted four months. He served in the Virginia Line

---

[139] Revolutionary War Pension File for Reuben Howell (S2327), National Archives Microfilm M804, Roll 1347. Hereafter referred to as S2327.

[140] Loudoun County, VA, Will Bk B:176.

[141] Loudoun County, VA, Will Bk G:217.

[142] S2327

as a second sergeant in the Company of Capt. Adam Vinsel and the
Regiment of Col. Andrew Russell.

Reuben was called back to service in August 1781 as a sergeant.
This time he served in Capt. John Lucket's Company and Col.
West's Regiment. During this 3-month enlistment, he participated
in the siege of Yorktown and witnessed the surrender there of
British troops under General Cornwallis. His unit helped march the
British prisoners to a ferry location on the Potomac River where he
was discharged. He stated that he had had discharge papers for
both periods of service, but had lost them both over the years.

Based on his testimony and the statements of character witnesses,
Reuben's application for a pension was approved. The certificate
dated 5 March 1833 shows that he was approved for a pension at
the rate of $35 a year.

There is documentation that Reuben Howell maintained a presence
in Loudoun County after the war. His name is found in Loudoun
County personal property tax lists from 1785 - 1795.[143] In 1785
he was listed next to his mother, Margaret, and his brother,
Benjamin. In 1787, he owned one horse. In all these records, his
name is spelled Reubin.

After the move to Ohio, Reuben is found as a 45+ head of
household in the 1820 Census.[144] Living with him was a 45+
female, probably his wife. The family also included two males, one
age 16-18 and the other 16-26. Rounding out the 5-member family
was a 16-26 year old female. The record also shows two members
of the family were engaged in agriculture, a fancy term for farming.

---

[143] Loudoun County, VA Personal Property Tax Lists, (1785, 1787-1789, 1791,
1795), Part 1: 1782-1787; Part 2: 1787-1797, Battalion 1, N. pag.

[144] 1820 federal census, population schedule, Salem Township, Columbiana
County, OH, p. 67.

We don't know who Reuben married or when. Like many of the earlier Howells in Loudoun County, a marriage record could not be found. A book of Loudoun County Marriages from 1757-1853, compiled by Mary Alice Wertz in 1985 was checked without success. Based on the maximum ages of either the son or daughter (age 25) found in the 1820 Census, Reuben and his wife would have been married by 1794/95, at the latest.

We don't know when Reuben Howell died, but he was most likely dead by 1840. His name does not appear in the Ohio Census Index for that year. In the 1840 index his name in Salem Township is replaced by a Henry Howell, possibly his son. His name also does not appear in the General Index to a Census of Pensioners for Revolutionary or Military Service - 1840 published by the Genealogical Society of the Mormon Church in 1974.

A letter to a genealogical society in Columbiana County, Ohio produced the following responses.[145] There is no will or estate for Reuben Howell; he does not appear on the 1838 Tax List; no tombstone found.

We have scant evidence of Reuben Howell's children. The only real evidence we have of them is the stroke tally made when the 1820 Census was taken. Based on that tally, we know that he had at least three children. He may have had more.

24   i.   Male,[3] born c1794-1804, Loudoun County, Virginia

25   ii.   Female, born c1794-1804, Loudoun County, Virginia..

26   iii.   Male, born c1801-1803, Loudoun County, Virginia.

---

[145] Columbiana County Chapter of the Ohio Genealogical Society, P.O. Box 635, Salem, OH 44460 to Richard Wallace, 11 May 1992. Original in possession of author Wallace.

9. Rachel[2] Howell (Hugh[1]) was one of two daughters listed in
Hugh Howell's will.[146] She is listed first, so the chances are that
she was the older daughter. Rachel was probably born either in
New Jersey or Virginia before her father's death in 1777.

Rachel Howell was listed twice in her father's 1804 estate
accounting.[147] The cash she received amounted to £18 and 12
shillings. Incidentally her name in the accounting was recorded as
Rachel Howell, so she had not married as yet.

When some of the Loudoun County Howells moved to Ohio in the
early 1800's, Rachel may have gone with them. Her brother,
Benjamin, settled in Belmont County, Flushing Township. When
the 1820 Census was taken, there was a 45+ Rachel Howell living
alone in Flushing Township.[148] This could very well be Hugh's
daughter. Admittedly, this evidence is circumstantial. Nearby were
Benjamin and other Howell relatives.

We do not know when Rachel Howell died. The last positive
evidence we have for her is the 1804 estate accounting. If she is
the Rachel Howell we found in the 1820 census, then she died after
that date.

10. Ann[2] Howell (Hugh[1]) was one of two daughters, listed as heirs
in the 1777 will of Hugh Howell.[149] Other than her name, we
know practically nothing about this child. She was born before
1777 and could have been born either in New Jersey or Virginia.

---

[146] Loudoun County, VA, Will Bk B:176.

[147] Loudoun County, VA, Will Bk G:217.

[148] 1820 federal census, population schedule, Belmont County, OH, p. 159.

[149] Loudoun County, VA, Will Bk B:176.

When her father's estate was settled in 1804, Ann was not mentioned as one of those receiving cash.[150] The accounting also does not mention any men, other than Howells, who received amounts that would suggest that one of them was Ann's husband. She may not have survived to adulthood. However, we simply don't know what happened to her after 1777.

---

[150] Loudoun County, VA, Will Bk G:217.

CHAPTER FOUR

CONTINUED MOVEMENT TO OHIO
GENERATION THREE

Son of Hugh

Three of William Howell's four children moved on to Ohio and settled there prior to 1820. Jesse, the eldest, did by one report, live in Ohio at one time, but no documentary evidence of his residing there could be found. He died in Loudoun County, Virginia. Abner went to Muskingum County, where he lived out his life. Abel went to nearby Belmont County where he spent the rest of his life. Margaret and her family settled in Guernsey County, which bordered on both Muskingum and Belmont Counties. However, sometime after the death of her husband, she spent her remaining days in Madison County where she lived with other relatives.

11. Jesse[3] Howell (William[2], Hugh[1]) was born 9 February 1770/1771/1772 in Shelburne Parish, Loudoun County, Virginia,[151] and died there on 1 February 1854.[152] He married Hannah James 10 June 1795 probably in Loudoun County. She was born 8 July 1772 in Loudoun County and died 10 December 1852 in Loudoun County.[153]

---

[151] DAR applicants Leona Cryer, #677790; Martha Irvin Newman, #418825; Estelle Howell Smith, #417368 are not in agreement on year of birth.

[152] Frances Jones to Robert Cameron, 30 December 1990.

[153] DAR applicants Estelle Howell Smith, #417368; Mary Irvin Newman, #418825.

Jesse first appeared in Loudoun County records on the tax list for 1789, living adjacent to his father, William.[154]   He also appeared in the 1810 and 1820 census in Loudoun County.[155]   Jesse served as administrator of his father's estate in 1817 and 1818, presenting an accounting at the Loudoun County Court 9 June 1818.[156] Jesse is mentioned in a deposition given by Samuel Marks in Henderson, Kentucky on 6 November 1832 concerning the pension application of Captain Isaiah Marks. Captain Marks was Jesse's uncle [brother to his mother, Martha Marks]. In the deposition, it listed, "a 2nd sister Patsy Howell, alias Marks, dead leaving Jesse, Abner, Abel & Margaret of the state of Ohio."[157]   If Jesse lived in Ohio, it must have been for a brief time between census records, for he could not be located there.

Jesse bought 102 acres in Loudoun County 16 December 1797 from Isaac James of Bedford County, Virginia. Witnesses included William Howell and Abel Howell, presumably his father and brother.[158]

As stated above, Jesse died in Loudoun County 1 February 1854 and an inventory and appraisement were taken by sons Craven and David and presented to the Court in April 1855. Final distribution of his estate, totaling $1836.84 was divided among seven legatees on 7 June

---

[154] Netti Schreiner-Yantis & Florence Love, <u>The Personal Property Tax Lists for the Year 1789 for Loudoun County, Virginia</u> (Springfield, VA: Genealogical Books in Print, 1986), p. 66.

[155] 1810 federal census, population schedule, Loudoun County, VA, p. 293; 1820 federal census, population schedule, Loudoun County, VA, p. 136A.

[156] Loudoun County, VA, Will Bk M:304.

[157] "Affidavit of Samuel Marks," Capt. Isaiah Marks Pension File #R16055, U.S. Revolutionary War Service, National Archives and Records Service, Washington, D.C., M804, roll 1631, p. 0032-0067. This information courtesy of Frances Jones.

[158] Loudoun County, VA, Deed Bk ???:159.

1856.[159]   Living descendants have recently [1991] been located in Round Hill, Loudoun County.[160]

Known children of Jesse and Hannah (James) Howell include:[161]

27   i.   Levi[4] Howell, born 10 July 1795, died 14 July 1795

28   ii.   Abel Howell, born 30 September 1796, died 25 October 1798.

29   iii.   Elijah Howell, born 14 December 1799; married Elizabeth.[162]

30   iv.   Anna Howell, born 6 January 1802.

31   v.   David Howell, born 17 September 1803; married Mahala.[163]

32   vi.   Craven James Howell, born 13 October 1805, died 14 January 1887; married, 5 November 1833, Amy W. McNight.[164]

---

[159] Loudoun County, VA, Will Bk 2L:136.

[160] Phyllis M. Darr, P.O. Box 55, Round Hill, VA 22141 to Carmen J. Finley, 18 September 1991. She had been married to Howard Thompson, son of Martha Howell Thompson, granddaughter of Jesse.

[161] Bible record found in the Flavious J. Howell Bible by Phyllis M. Darr; copy in possession of writer, gives all birth and some death dates.

[162] Estelle Howell Smith to N.S.D.A.R. Registrar General, Mrs. Kenneth Troy Trewhella, 6 April 1953.

[163] Estelle Howell Smith to Mrs. Kenneth Troy Trewhella.

[164] Margaret E. Myers, Marriage Licenses of Frederick County, 1811-1840 (Silver Spring, MD: Family Line Publications, 1987), p. 120.

33   vii.   Eda/Edah (Edith) Howell, born 16 December 1807; married, 24 September 1832, Washington Jenkins.[165]

34   viii.   Emily Howell, born 6 August 1810; married, 5 May 1846, Norval V. Heskett.[166]

35   ix.   James M. Howell, born 23 January 1813; married Martha C. Huffman.[167]

12. Abner[3] Howell (William[2], Hugh[1]) was born 27 August 1775 in Loudoun County, Virginia[168] and died 17 September 1841 in Muskingum County, Ohio.[169] He probably did marry, as other researchers have concluded, Priscilla Wade, the daughter of Daniel and Mary Wade, 16 February 1801.[170] The authors did not find any evidence that Abner ever lived in Fauquier County, but he did live near the Fauquier County line, close to the area where Daniel Wade

---

[165] Mary Alice Wertz, <u>Marriages of Loudoun County</u> (Baltimore: Genealogical Publishing, 1985), p. 82.

[166] Ibid., p. 70.

[167] Estelle Howell Smith to Mrs. Kenneth Troy Trewhella.

[168] Family bible records of Abner Howell, Jr. in possession of Mae (Kennedy) Morris, Rt. 1, Kimbolton, OH 43749 great granddaughter of Abner's son, Abner, Jr. Copies in possession of the authors.

[169] Muskingum County, OH, Administration Docket, B:110, case #1904, LDS film #865159.

[170] Nancy Chappelear & John K. Gott, <u>Fauquier County, Virginia Marriage Bonds</u> (Washington, D.C.: author, 1965), p. 62.

lived.[171] Priscilla Wade was probably born 1780 to 1790 and died probably between 1830 and 1840, probably in Muskingum County, Ohio.[172] Abner married (2) Isabella McCracken 2 April 1841.[173] Isabella was born about 1793/94 in Pennsylvania, according to the 1860 census when she was found living with Abner's son, Alfred.[174]

After his first marriage, Abner continued living in Loudoun County, where we found him living with his father, William, in 1799.[175] That year they were taxed on the ownership of five horses. Living nearby was Timothy Howell's widow, Rebecca, and brother Jesse.

Abner was found in Loudoun County records 5 June 1818 when he was listed in the estate settlement of his father, William. In that accounting he received money for "keeping his father and mother," and an additional $80 "in part of his legacy."[176] 1850 census records say that his first nine children were born in Virginia between 1803 and

---

[171] Phyllis T. Scott, 6449 Rattle Branch Road, Marshall, VA 22115 to Richard Wallace, 11 December 1992 and 8 February 1993. Originals in possession of author Wallace.

[172] 1830 census shows one adult female age 40-50; 1840 census shows oldest female age 20-30. Federal census, population schedules, Rich Hill Township, Muskingum County, OH, p. 261, 485 respectively.

[173] Muskingum County Ohio, Marriage Book #3, 1835-1848, (Zanesville, OH: Muskingum County Chapter, Ohio Genealogical Society, 1982) p. 15.

[174] 1860 federal census, population schedule, Rich Hill Township, Muskingum County, p. 111, dwelling #792, family #792.

[175] Loudoun County Personal Property Tax List (1799), Part 3: 1798-1812, Battalion 1, N. pag., microfilmed by Virginia State Library, Richmond, VA. Copy available at Thomas Balch Library, Local History Room, Leesburg, VA.

[176] Loudoun County, VA, Will Bk M:304.

1817,[177] although there is some confusion as to the birth place of the ninth child, George, since the 1860 census says George was born in Ohio.[178] But Margaret, Abner's tenth child, was born in Muskingum County, 2 May 1818. Abner's first, and only, land purchase in Muskingum County, Ohio was made 1 June 1826 from the United States ... the southwest quarter of section 26, township 13, range 11, containing 163.26 acres.[179] This was located about 20 miles from Zanesville where he staked his claim at the local land office. On 17 April 1841, Abner and his new wife, Isabella, sold 40 acres of this to Abner's son, Alfred.[180]

Although the precise time of Abner's arrival in Muskingum County is unclear, it was most likely during the period 1817 to early 1818, even though he did not appear in the 1820 census in Ohio. That year a Priscilla Howell, possibly our Priscilla, is listed as a member of John Crawford's "class" at the Salem Methodist Church in Muskingum County, Ohio - Salem Township.[181] Loudoun County land tax records for 1816 show him leasing 116 acres on Little River located 15 miles southwest of the Courthouse.[182] This land had apparently

---

[177] 1850 OH federal census, population schedule, Rich Hill Township, Muskingum County, p. 480, dwelling #135, family #135; p. 484, dwelling #194, family #194; Highland Township, p. 422, dwelling #928, family #934; Percy Township, Muskingum County, p. 362, dwelling #104, family #104; Hopewell Township, p. 88, dwelling #289, family #290; Swan Township, Vinton County, p. 654, dwelling #150, family #151; p. 654, dwelling #152, family #153; Benton Township, Hocking County, p. 437, dwelling #190, family #192.

[178] 1860 federal census, population schedule, Swan Township, Vinton County, OH, p. 294, dwelling #441, family #333.

[179] Muskingum County, OH, Deed Bk 42:257.

[180] Muskingum County, OH, Deed Bk 1:124.

[181] History of Muskingum County, Ohio (Columbus, OH: J.F. Everhart & Co., 1882), p. 447.

[182] Loudoun County, VA, Land Tax Records, District C, 1816. Microfilmed by Virginia State Library, Richmond, VA.

Vol. 42
pg. 257

Received June 1, 1864
Recorded June 27, 1864

United States
to
Abner Howell

3840.

John Quincy Adams, President of the United States of America. To all to whom these presents shall come, greeting: Know ye, That Abner Howell of Muskingum County Ohio, having deposited in the general land office, a certificate of the Register of the Land office at Zanesville whereby it appears that full payment has been made for the south west quarter of section twenty of the Township Thornton of Range eleven, containing one hundred and sixty three acres t twenty one hundredths of an acre of the lands directed to be sold at Zanesville by the act of Congress entitled "An act providing for the sale of the lands of the United States in the territory north west of the Ohio, and above the mouth of Kentucky River, and of the act amendatory of the same, there is granted by the United States unto the said Abner Howell and to his heirs the quarter lot or section of land above described: To have and to hold the said quarter lot or section of land, with the appurtenances, unto the said Abner Howell & to his heirs and assigns forever. In testimony whereof I have caused these letters to be made Patent and the seal of the general land office to be hereunto affixd. Given under my hand at the city of Washington the first day of January in the year of our Lord one thousand eight hundred and twenty six and of the independence of the United States of America the fiftieth.

By the President

J. Q. Adams

G. F. Graham, Commissioner of the General Land office.

Recorded in Volume 54 Page 61.

Abner Howell, grandson of Hugh and Margaret, relocated in Muskingum County, Ohio before 1820 and received this grant for 163+ acres in 1826.

been leased earlier to William Howell. By 1818, this same land had been leased again from Abner to Jesse Howell, suggesting that Abner was getting ready to move to Ohio.[183] Abner and his family may well have taken the same route from Loudoun County as his cousin, John Howell, did in 1806. They floated down the Monongahela in a flatboat and landed opposite Wheeling, then proceeded westward to a cabin near Flushing in Belmont County, a scant 35 miles northeast of where Abner settled. When Abner arrived, Ohio was still a new state having been admitted to the Union in 1803. It was still very much frontier country when Abner arrived. In 1796, Colonel Ebenezer Zane had bargained with the United States Senate and House of Representatives to cut a trace from Wheeling to Maysville, Kentucky. Two years later, there was a trace wide enough for a mail rider. That encouraged others to travel and widen the route. By 1817, Zanesville had 1250 people, 176 horses, 2 stone houses, 35 brick and 13 wooden houses and some log cabins, 5 schools, 2 banks, 7 taverns, 16 stores and 3 glass factories. By 1832, with further improvements to the roads and bridges of what later became US Highway 40, traffic increased to 35,310 men on horseback, 16,750 horses, 24,410 sheep, 52,845 hogs, 96,323 cattle, 14,907 one-horse carriages, 11,613 two-horse wagons and 2,357 three-horse wagons.[184] Rich Hill Township, where Abner and his family lived, was organized in 1815 and is today, essentially an agricultural district. This area has experienced considerable coal strip mining and currently is destined to be the site of a wild animal theme park. Andrew Howell (no proven relationship to date) built the first frame house in Rich Hill Township 1819. His farm was about 4 miles northwest of Abner's.[185]

[183] Loudoun County, VA, Land Tax Records, District C, 1818. Microfilmed by Virginia State Library, Richmond, VA.

[184] J.H. Newton, ed., History of Belmont And Jefferson County, Ohio (Wheeling, WV: Historical Publishing Co., 1880), p. 380.

[185] Biographical and Historical Memoirs of Muskingum County, Ohio (Chicago: Goodspeed Publishing, 1892), p. 351.

*Record of births of Abner Howell's children, found in the Bible
of Abner Howell, Jr.*

Abner with his family was found in the 1830 and 1840 census in Rich
Hill Township, Muskingum County.[186]   Abner died the next year,
intestate, 17 September 1841, presumably in Rich Hill Township.
George Holmes, Abner's son-in-law, who had married Mary Ann,
served as administrator.[187]   A series of six land records between 15
March 1844 and 1 July 1847 plus a court record, accounted for 13

---

[186] 1830 and 1840 federal census, population schedule, Rich Hill Township,
Muskingum County, OH, p. 261, 485 respectively.

[187] Muskingum County, OH, 1830-61, Administration Docket, B:110, case
#1904. Also LDS film #865159.

undivided shares of Abner's estate and named all children except Madison, the youngest.[188]

Known children of Abner and Priscilla (Wade) Howell included the following:[189]

+36   i.   James[4] Howell, born 1 January 1803, Virginia.

+37   ii.   Alfred Howell, born 10 April 1804, Virginia.

+38   iii.   Martha Howell, born 10 March 1807, Virginia.

+39   iv.   Elizabeth Howell, 10 December 1808, Virginia.

+40   v.   Amanda Howell, born 29 June 1810, Virginia.

+41   vi.   Frances (Fanny) Howell, born 2 October 1812, Virginia.

+42   vii.   Urey Howell, born 9 August 1813, Virginia.

+43   viii.   Mary Ann Howell, born 20 October 1815, Virginia.

+44   ix.   George Howell, born 8 September 1817, Virginia or Ohio.

+45   x.   Margaret Howell, born 2 May 1818, Rix Mill, Muskingum County, Ohio.

+46   xi.   John Howell, born 9 March 1820, Ohio.

---

[188] Muskingum County, OH, Deed Book, 10:14, 13:5-7; 18:453, Appointment Docket S 1846-1848, April Term 1847.

[189] Family Bible Records of Abner Howell, Jr.

+47   xii.   Abner Howell, born 11 May 1824, Rich Hill
                     Township,   Muskingum County, Ohio.

+48   xiii.   Madison Howell, born 2 September 1826,
                     Muskingum County, Ohio.

13. Abel[3] Howell (William[2], Hugh[1]) was born 28 December 1778[190] in Virginia.[191]   He was probably born in the northern part of Virginia in Loudoun County.   He died in 1854,[192] probably in Flushing Township, Belmont County, Ohio and is buried at Rock Hill Church Cemetery in Flushing Township, Belmont County.[193]   Abel is listed as an heir in the estate settlement of his father.[194]   He married, probably in Virginia, Naomi Reed[195] who was born in 1774/1775[196] in Virginia,[197] and died 1872[198] probably in Flushing Township, Belmont County. Her parents are unknown. She is buried beside her husband.

---

[190] Esther Weygant Powell, Tombstone Inscriptions and Family Records of Belmont County, Ohio (Akron, OH: author, 1969), p. 17. Also family Bible held (in 1953) by Ina Merchant, Charles Town, Jefferson County, WV.

[191] 1850 federal census, population schedule, Flushing Township, Belmont County, OH, p. 170, dwelling #888, family #902.

[192] Powell, Tombstone Inscriptions, p. 17.

[193] Ibid., p. 16.

[194] Loudoun County, VA, Will Bk M:304.

[195] DAR application of Estelle Howell Smith.

[196] Powell, Tombstone Inscriptions, p. 16.

[197] 1850 census noted above.

[198] Powell, Tombstone Inscriptions, p. 17.

A document which helps to identify Abel is an 1832 Henderson County, Kentucky deposition which specifies his mother and siblings and which indicates an Ohio residence.[199] Another document is a sheet of paper tucked in the family bible of Flavious J. Howell.[200] The last line on that sheet reads: "Jessie Howell's Brothers are in Bell Mount County, Ohio."

The 1810 Virginia census shows an Abel Howell with the number of individuals in each of the age and gender categories matching the ages and genders of our Abel's family.[201] Furthermore that same census record shows a Jesse Howell (whose statistics match Jesse's family) just two lines above Abel's record. It is quite likely that this is our Abel.

Evidence of the time of arrival of Abel and Naomi in Ohio is displayed in the Ohio 1850 census where it shows Ohio as the birth place of their daughter, Neoma (who was born 16 December 1812 according to Esther Weygant Powell[202] and the month and year verified by the 1900 census).[203] Censuses subsequent to the 1850 census also verify that birthplace. Furthermore, this 1850 census shows their son, Israel, who was born 1810/1812 as having been born in Virginia. Consequently, it can be deduced that the family arrived in Ohio during the period from 1810 to 1812. This time of arrival coincides with a land patent granted to Abel Howell, a resident of Belmont County, on 11 July 1811 for property in Section 25 of

---

[199] Affidavit of Samuel Marks.

[200] Phyllis M. Darr to Carmen J. Finley.

[201] 1810 federal census, population schedule, Loudoun County, VA, p. 293A.

[202] Powell, Tombstone Inscriptions, p. 16.

[203] 1900 federal census, population schedule, Union Township, Belmont County, OH, sheet 192B, dwelling #170, family #170. Enumerated with family of Nancy Haines, 57 year old widow, where Naomi was shown as a boarder.

Township 9 in Range 5.[204]   That property lies at the south edge of
what is currently Flushing Township near the village of Flushing.
This would have been about four to six years after Abel's first cousin,
John Howell, son of Benjamin departed Loudoun County, Virginia for
Belmont County, Ohio.

The 1820 census[205] shows Abel in Flushing Township of Belmont
County as head of household with a total of 5 males and 6 females.
The statistics of this census fit in nicely with the children listed below.

Checking the 1830 census, we find a 50-60 year old Abel Howell as
head of household living with a 60-70 year old female and two other
males (one 10 to 15 and one 15-20) and five other females (one 0-5,
two 10-15, one 20-30, and one 30-40).[206]

The 1850 census lists the following people: Abel, aged 72, Virginia
native; 70 year old Neoma, a Virginia native; 40-year old Virginia
native, Margaret (their daughter); 38-year old Virginia native, Israel
(their son); 31-year old Ohio native, Menona (their daughter); 27-year
old Ohio native, Unice (their daughter); 5-year old Ohio native, Hester
A. (Israel's daughter); and 2-year old Ohio native, Allice I.   Also
living with them was a 26-year old Ohio native, James Humphrey (the
future husband of Unice).[207]

Abel died in 1854.[208]   In his will,[209]   prepared 13 September 1852

---

[204] Carol Willsey Bell, <u>Ohio Lands: Steubenville Land Office, 1800-1820</u>
(Youngstown, OH: author, 1984), p. 82. This information was extracted from
Certificate #3339 of page 119, Vol. 432 of the original record.

[205] 1820 federal census, population schedule, Flushing Township, Belmont
County, OH, p. 157.

[206] 1830 federal census, population schedule, Flushing Township, Belmont
County, OH, p. 327.

[207] 1850 federal census, population schedule, Flushing Township, Belmont
County, OH, p. 171, dwelling #888, family #902.

[208] Powell, <u>Tombstone Inscriptions</u>, p. 16.

and filed for probate 11 February 1854, he left a life estate to his "beloved wife" (not named). After her death, he provided for the bulk of his estate to go to his son Israel. He directed Israel to make cash bequests to his other children, namely Jesse, William, Abel, Miner, Nancy, Margaret, Naomi, Hester, and Eunice. Martha, a child mentioned in the Bible fragment, is not named. It can be speculated that she died before her father died.

In the 1860 census Naomi is shown as an 82-year old Virginia native living in Flushing Township with her son, Israel.[210] Her daughter, Margaret, also resided there. As stated above, Naomi died in 1872.[211]

Since Abel Howell, Jr., lived in the vicinity of his father one must be careful to assure that the data on the two Abels are not confused.[212] Abel Howell, Jr.'s wife, Catherine, is buried in Rock Hill Cemetery,[213] the same cemetery where members of our family were buried. Even though no person by the name of Able was included as a child of Abel and Naomi in the bible record, an Abel was shown as an heir in the will.

A land patent shows that an Abel Howell, a resident of Belmont County, purchased land 12 May 1815.[214] Since Abel, Jr. was then too young to own property the patent must have been obtained by Abel, Sr. However, subsequent census data would suggest that Abel,

---

[209] Belmont County, OH, Will Bk H, pp. 359-360.

[210] 1860 federal census, population schedule, Flushing Township, Belmont County, OH, p. 129, dwelling #1764, family #1772.

[211] Powell, Tombstone Inscriptions, p. 17.

[212] 1860 federal census, population schedule, Harrison County, Moorefield Township, Moorefield P.O., p. 159, dwelling #52, family #51.

[213] Powell, Tombstone Inscriptions, p. 16.

[214] Charles A. Hanna, Historical Collections of Harrison County in the State of Ohio (New York, 1900), p. 217.

Jr. occupied this land.   This was the SW quarter of Section 23,
Township 9 of Range 5.   This lies in Moorefield Township, Harrison
County.   This was land located in the "Seven Ranges."   The Seven
Ranges were the first land surveyed by government surveyors under
the Continental Congress, and the townships were numbered according
to the Land Ordinance of 20 May 1785.[215]   Township 9 of this
original survey overlaps parts of the present Moorefield Township in
Harrison County and Flushing Township of Belmont County.   The
data from the census cited above would suggest that this 1813 Land
Patent was obtained by this "other" Abel Howell.   The dwellings of
these two Abel Howells were less than 5 miles apart.

A person by the name of Abel Howell purchased from the
Steubenville Land Office property in Range XI, Township 10, Section
17 on 17 May 1831.[216]   He was a resident of Belmont County.   The
property is near Freeport in the southwest corner of the adjacent
Harrison County.

Abel's will which is cited above is the primary source to verify the
known children (except for Martha as discussed above) of Abel and
Naomi. The page, mentioned above, tucked in the Flavious J. Howell
Bible[217] lists seven of the eleven children but fails to list Abel,
Margaret, Hester and Unice:

49   i.   Abel[4] Howell, born 1803/1804 in Virginia; married
                   12 April 1827 in Belmont County, Ohio, Catherine
                   Lamma.[218]

50   ii.   Jesse Howell, born 1800/1810, in Virginia.

---

[215] Thomas Aquinas Burke, Ohio Lands--A Short History (Columbus, OH: Ohio
State Auditor, 1987), p. 11.

[216] Hanna, Historical Collections of Harrison County, p. 217.

[217] Phyllis M. Darr to Carmen J. Finley.

[218] International Genealogical Index (IGI), LDS, Ohio, Batch 7931802.

| 51 | iii. | William Howell, born 1800/1810, in Virginia. |

| 52 | iv. | Margaret Howell, born 1808/1809[219] in Virginia, died 1873 in Belmont County, Ohio.[220] |

| 53 | v. | Israel Howell, born 1810/1812 in Virginia,[221] married (second wife) 3 July 1856 in Belmont County, Ohio, Mary Cecill. |

| 54 | vi. | Neoma Howell, born 16 December 1812 in Ohio, married 21 May 1855, Absalom Yonally (his third wife),[222] died 1904.[223] |

| 55 | vii. | Hester Howell, born 1813,[224] married 30 January 1837 William Humphrey in Belmont County,[225] died 1875.[226] |

---

[219] 1850 federal census, population schedule, Flushing Township, Belmont County, OH, p. 170, dwelling #888, family #902.

[220] Powell, Tombstone Inscriptions, p. 16.

[221] 1850 federal census, population schedule, Flushing Township, Belmont County, OH, p. 170, dwelling #888, family #902.

[222] Ohio Extension Homemakers, Belmont County, Belmont County History, 1988 (Salem, WV: Wadsworth Press, Inc., Don Mills, Inc.), p. 303.

[223] Powell, Tombstone Inscriptions, p. 16.

[224] Ibid. p. 13.

[225] International Genealogical Index (IGI), LDS, Ohio.

[226] Powell, Tombstone Inscriptions, p. 13.

56	viii.	Miner Howell, born 1819/1820 in Ohio,[227] married 24 January 1843 in Flushing, Belmont County, Martha Williams.[228]
57	ix.	Unice Howell, born 1822/23 in Ohio, married 27 April 1854 in Belmont County, James Humphrey.[229]
58	x.	Nancy Howell.
59	xi.	Martha Howell.

14. The only known daughter of William and Martha (Marks) Howell was Margaret. By most accounts, Margaret[3] Howell (William[2], Hugh[1]) was born 2 September 1782, probably in Loudoun County, Virginia.[230] She died 16 September 1871, in Madison County, Ohio. She married Thomas West, born 1770/80, 10 September 1798,[231] probably in Loudoun County, Virginia. Thomas probably died in Guernsey County, Ohio between the census years of 1840 and 1850.

We do not know what proofs the DAR applicants used to justify their conclusion, but we found good evidence to support Margaret's year of

---

[227] 1880 federal census, population schedule, Union Township, Belmont County, p. 414A, dwelling #325, family #327.

[228] International Genealogical Index (IGI), LDS, Ohio.

[229]Ibid.

[230] DAR applicants Jessie C. Tomlinson, Estelle H. Smith, Barbara E. Herring, and Mary I. Newman.

[231] John Voght & T. William Kethy, Jr., Virginia Historic Marriage Register - Loudoun County Marriages, 1760-1850 (Athens, GA: Iberian Publishing, 1985), p. 308.

birth. In 1850, a 68-year old Margaret West, native of Virginia, was living with her son, William West, in Washington County, Ohio.[232]

A hand-written note that was found in a Howell Bible contains important information on Margaret Howell.[233] The note mentions, "Jessie Able Abner Marget Howell Brothers & sistr." Another part of the note states, "Jessie Ephern Walice are the suns of Tomas West married Marget Howell Sister of Jessie Howell." The obvious spelling and grammatical errors in this note are more than mitigated by the information it reveals.

When William Howell's estate was settled in 1818,[234] Thomas West received $80 in cash as part of his legacy.

The whereabouts of Thomas and Margaret West after their marriage has been a matter of some speculation. West is a common surname so it is not difficult to find a Thomas West. In fact 10 were found in Virginia in 1810, but none were living in Loudoun County. There was a Thomas West living in Jefferson County, Virginia.[235] This is the county directly northwest of Loudoun County. However, the oldest female in this 4-member family was only age 16-26, a little young to be Margaret. Also the head of household is over 45 years old - probably too old to be Margaret's husband. Based on the Bible note, Thomas and Margaret had at least three sons. This household has only one son under 10 years of age.

Another Thomas West was found in Monongalia County, Virginia in 1810.[236] The age configuration for this family is as follows:

---

[232] 1850 federal census, free schedule, Ludlow Township, Washington County, OH, p. 997, dwelling #99, family #99.

[233] Phyllis M. Darr to Carmen J. Finley.

[234] Loudoun County, VA, Will Bk M:304.

[235] Jackson & Peoples, Virginia 1810 Census Index, p. 170.

[236] Ibid., p. 441.

Table 1. Thomas West Family,
Monongalia County, Virginia, 1810

Sex	<10	26-44
Males	2	1
Females	3	1

The configuration looks better for this family, but we cannot be certain that this is the right family.

As for the eight other Thomas Wests we found, they did not live near the normal migration routes from Loudoun County. Most were living in eastern or southeastern Virginia.

A clue to the eventual whereabouts of Thomas and Margaret can be found in a 6 November 1832 Henderson County, Kentucky court appearance by Samuel Marks.[237] He was the nephew of Martha Marks Howell and cousin of Margaret Howell West. In this court deposition which details the heirs of Capt. Isaiah Marks, deceased, he refers to a "2nd sister Patsey [Martha] Howell, alias Marks, dead leaving Jesse, Abner, Able & Margaret of the state of Ohio."

Checking the 1840 Ohio Census, we find a 60-70 year old farmer, Thomas West, living in Guernsey County, Wills Township.[238] This county is sandwiched between Belmont and Muskingum County, where we already know other Howell relatives located. Living with him was a 50-60 year old female, 3 persons in the 20-30 age group (2 males and 1 female), and one male age 10-15.

---

[237] Affidavit of Samuel Marks.

[238] 1840 federal census, population schedule, Willis Township, Guernsey County, OH, p. 312.

In the same county and township is a Wallace West, age 30-40[239] and an Eber West, age 30-40.[240] Both were farmers. A 20-30 year old Thomas West was living in Guernsey County, Seneca Township.[241]

The National Road, which passes directly through Wills Township, replaced Zane's Trace, which was merely a blazed trail through the unbroken wilderness.[242] It ran north of Zane's Trace, and it was a much better route to travel. This information makes it easier to understand how the Wests and other settlers happened to settle in Wills Township.

Another reason settlers found themselves in Wills Township was the price of land. Wills Township was located in the U.S. Military District where land prices were several cents an acre cheaper than in the land grant known as the Seven Ranges - east of Wills Township.[243] Land prices in the Seven Ranges sold mostly for $2 an acre.

The Thomas West who lived in Guernsey County, Ohio in 1840 is probably also the one who lived there in 1820.[244] That year there was an age 45+ Thomas West and an age 45+ female living there. With them were 5 children under 10 (3 were males), 3 males 10-15, and 1 female 16-26. The 45+ female would at first seem to be too old, based on the DAR applications and the 1850 census record, to be Margaret.

---

[239] Ibid., p. 305.

[240] Ibid., p. 305.

[241] Ibid., p. 422.

[242] William G. Wolfe, Stories of Guernsey County, Ohio (Cambridge, OH: author, 1943), p. 1063.

[243] Ibid., p. 1054.

[244] 1820 federal census, population schedule, Guernsey County, OH, p. 179.

Adding weight to the conclusion that our Thomas and Margaret West moved to Guernsey County is the fact that they together sold 160 acres there, 120 acres in 1818[245] and 40 acres in 1823.[246] Both sales were in Section 15, Township 2, Range 1. Also we found a marriage record there for Wallace West,[247] whose full name was William Wallace West. He married Elizabeth Ward on 12 January 1837. This was probably not a first marriage for William, who we think had a son born about 1830 (see note under William Wallace West following).

We do not know exactly when Thomas West died, but it was probably between the census years 1840 - 1850. An estate record for a Thomas West could not be found in Guernsey County for applicable periods. He was not listed with Margaret in the 1850 census record we referenced at the beginning of this section.

By 1860 Margaret West was no longer living with son, William, who had moved to Monroe County, Ohio.[248] She had gone to live with other relatives in Madison County, Ohio. We found the 77-year old Virginia native living there in June 1860.[249] Living with her was a 47-year old Rosanna West, a 19-year old Rachel West and a 1-year old Mary Jane Cannady, all natives of Ohio. Living in the same dwelling but listed as a separate family was a 35-year old Amelia West and five younger Wests ranging in age from 8 to 17.[250]

---

[245] Guernsey County, OH, Deed Bk C:283.

[246] Guernsey County, OH, Deed Bk D:258.

[247] Guernsey County, OH, Marriage Bk C:182.

[248] 1860 federal census, population schedule, Bethel Township, Monroe County, OH, p. 272, dwelling #601, family #601. Living next door to William was brother, Eber West, who had moved to Monroe County from Guernsey County.

[249] 1860 federal census, population schedule, Somerford Township, Madison County, OH, p. 329, dwelling #425, family #459.

[250] Ibid., dwelling #426, family #460.

Living two dwellings away, we found a 51-year old Alexander West (Margaret's son?) and a 48-year old Elisabeth West, along with seven West children.[251] Margaret West continued to live in Madison County until her death, which occurred 16 September 1871, at age 89. Her death record shows that she was living in Somerford Township.[252]

Based on the Bible note previously mentioned, Thomas and Margaret had at least three children as follows:

60   i.   Ephern (Ephraim/Eber)[4] West, born 1802/03[253] in Virginia.

61   ii.   William Wallace West, born 1805/06, Virginia.[254]

62   iii.   Jesse[4] West, born 1819/20 in Ohio[255].

Based on census data, they may also have had as many as 6 other children whose names we are not certain of.

---

[251] Ibid., dwelling #423, family #457.

[252] Ruth Bowers & Anita Short, comp. "Madison County, Ohio Death Records 1871-1875," Vol. 2 of <u>Gateway to the West</u> (Baltimore: Genealogical Publishing Co., 1978), p. 49.

[253] 1850 federal census, free schedule, Wills Township, Guernsey County, OH, p. 220-221, dwelling #1210, family #1214. This record shows Eber West, age 47, born in VA. Also shown are Lydia, age 36, and nine children.

[254] 1850 federal census, free schedule, Ludlow Township, Washington County, OH, p. 997, dwelling #99, family #99. This record shows Virginia native William West, age 44; his mother; Martha Delong, age 35 (sister?); 4 Delong children; and William West, age 20. Guernsey County Marriage Bk C:289 shows Martha West married Simpson Delong 5 December 1839.

[255] 1850 federal census, free schedule, Wills Township, Guernsey County, OH, p. 227, dwelling #1291, family #1294. This record shows Jesse West, age 30, born in Ohio. Also shown are "Margary," age 32, and four children.

17. John[3] Howell (Benjamin[2], Hugh[1]) was born 13 January 1784 in Loudoun County, Virginia[256] and died 10 June 1844[257] in Flushing Township, Belmont County, Ohio, and is buried at Windy Point Cemetery, Flushing Township, Belmont County.[258] He married Eleanor Mercer, daughter of John and Lydia (Barrett) Mercer.[259] [260] Eleanor was born 6 June 1792[261] and died 6 September 1873[262], and is buried beside her husband.[263] John and Lydia (Barrett) Mercer settled in Belmont County between 1805 and 1810.[264] Lydia was a Quaker and was disowned by her church when she married John, who was not a Quaker[265].

The History of Belmont and Jefferson Counties,[266] when describing John's fifth child, Hiram, said:

> His father emigrated from Loudoun County, Va., in 1805 and located about one and a half miles south of present town of Flushing; returned in the spring of 1806 and brought his father's family out. Floating

---

[256] Johnson, The Howell Family History, p. 2.

[257] Ibid, p. 2.

[258] Powell, Tombstone Inscriptions, p. 13.

[259] Johnson, The Howell Family History, p. 6.

[260] Frederick Barrett Emery, M.D., Barrett Family, Concordia, Kansas, 1955. Microfilmed by Latter Day Saints [US/CAN FILM AREA, 0441493, item 8.]

[261] Johnson, The Howell Family History, p. 2.

[262] Ibid, p. 2.

[263] Powell, Tombstone Inscriptions, p. 13.

[264] Johnson, The Howell Family History, p. 6.

[265] Ibid.

[266] J. A. Caldwell, History of Belmont and Jefferson Counties, Ohio, p. 380.

down the Monongahela in a flatboat they landed
opposite Wheeling, and proceeded westward to occupy
the cabin prepared for them. Hiram was born on the
old homestead, and still occupies a portion of the
original entry.

The Belmont County History,[267] in its description of a descendant
of John's said:

> Donald was born of a pioneer family, a direct
> descendant of John Howell b. 1784 and Eleanor Mercer
> b 1792. John emigrated from Loudon Co., Va. to
> Belmont Co in 1805 to 1/2 mile south of Flushing. He
> floated down the Monongahela and Ohio River on a
> flatboat landing opposite Wheeling, W. Va. and going
> westward to build a cabin. He took up quarter sections
> of land direct from government grants signed by James
> Madison President and James Monroe--one in 1811 and
> one in 1812.

Known children of John and Eleanor (Mercer) Howell include the
following, all born in Flushing Township, Belmont County:[268]

+63   i.   Benjamin[4] Howell, born 8 March 1812.

64   ii.   Isaac Howell, born 16 March 1814.

65   iii.   Melinda Howell, born 12 December 1816.

66   iv.   Lemuel Howell, born 5 June 1819.

67   v.   Hiram D. Howell, born 18 April 1822.

---

[267] Ohio Extnsion Homemakers, Belmont County History, 1988, p. 127.

[268] Johnson, The Howell Family History, p. 3.

68   vi.   Emily Howell, born 3 February 1825.

69   vii.   Ingabee Howell, born about 1828.

70   viii.   Rhoda Howell, born 30 January 1830.

71   ix.   John Howell, born 18 January 1832.

72   x.   Lydia Ann Howell, born 18 December 1834.

CHAPTER FIVE

CHILDREN OF ABNER³ AND JOHN³
GENERATION FOUR

Most of Abner's children lived, at least for a while, in Ohio after attaining adulthood. At least two of them, George and Madison, moved on to Missouri, with their families where they spent the remainder of their lives. Benjamin Howell, son of John, the only other fourth generation Howell studied, was born and died in Ohio.

36. James⁴ Howell (Abner³, William², Hugh¹), the oldest child of Abner and Priscilla (Wade) Howell, was probably born in Loudoun County, Virginia 11 January 1803.[269] He probably died between the census years of 1850 and 1860. He married Eliza Mowry 7 December 1837 in Muskingum County.[270] The marriage record shows his surname as Howel.

When his father died, James' name appears in several of the legal transactions that were required to dispose of Abner's estate. James and his wife Eliza were among the signatories who quitclaimed 163.26 acres of land to brother Alfred on 15 March 1844.[271] Their names also appear in an 1847 petition to sell land in Muskingum County.[272]

---

[269] Family Bible Records of Abner Howell, Jr.

[270] Muskingum County, Ohio Marriage Book #3, 1835-1848 (Zanesville, OH: Muskingum County Chapter, Ohio Genealogical Society, 1982), p. 15.

[271] Muskingum County, OH, Deed Bk 18:452.

[272] Muskingum County, OH, Appointment Docket S (1846-1848), p. 400.

On 17 September 1850, James and Eliza Howell were living in Muskingum County, Highland Township, where James was farming.[273] The census of that date gives James' age as 45 and his birthplace as Virginia. Eliza's age is recorded as 29 and her birthplace as Ohio.

In 1860, Eliza Howell was still living in Highland Township, but James is not listed with her.[274] This fact is the basis for our earlier suggestion that he probably died before 1860. Eliza was living in the family of Thomas Mowrer, age 35, possibly her brother. The name Mowrer is very close to the spelling of her name on her 1837 marriage record. We have no further information on this family after the 1860 census.

The only known child of James and Eliza Howell, taken from the two census records, is as follows:

73   i.   John[5] F. (A?) Howell, born 1844/45 in Muskingum County, Ohio.

37.   Alfred[4] Howell (Abner[3], William[2], Hugh[1]) was born 10 April 1804[275] in Virginia[276] and died in 1900 during the period between June 1 and December 31. His gravestone shows the year of death only (1900). He married (1) Safronia Edna Prouty, daughter of Daniel and

---

[273] 1850 federal census, population schedule, Highland Township, Muskingum Co., OH, p. 422, dwelling #928, family #934.

[274] 1860 federal census, population schedule, Highland Township, Muskingum Co., OH, p. 473, dwelling #503, family #476.

[275] Family Bible Records of Abner Howell, Jr.

[276] 1850 federal census, population schedule, Rich Hill Township, Muskingum County, OH, page 484 (stamped) and 967 (written), dwelling #194, family #194.

Sarah (Goodale) Prouty,[277] [278] 8 April 1830, in Morgan County, Ohio.[279] She was born about June 1810 in Massachusetts,[280] probably in Holden, Worcester County. She probably died in 1860 after the June census.[281] Since Alfred was remarried on 22 August of the next year it is quite likely she died in 1860. Alfred married (2) Rachel Hamilton,[282] born 1824 in Perry Township, Muskingum County, Ohio and died 27 September 1889 in Rich Hill, Muskingum Co., Ohio. Her parents are unknown. She and Alfred are both buried in Mount Zion Cemetery, Rich Hill Township, Muskingum County.

The 1900 census indicates that he was born in April 1803. Another census in 1860 implies he was born in 1805. His position relative to the birth of his siblings and the predominant ages shown in the censuses support the conclusion that his birth year was 1804. His place of birth, Virginia, was ascertained from various census records beginning with 1850 and ending 1900.

---

[277] Leon A. Goodale, Notes on the Lives of Edward and Sarah Temple Goodale, pioneer settlers of Shrewsbury, Massachusetts, 1738-1786 (n.p.: n. pub., n.d.), p. 32.

[278] George E. Williams, A Genealogy of the Descendants of Robert Goodale/Goodell of Salem, Mass. (West Hartford, CT: author, 1984), p. 135.

[279] International Genealogical Index (IGI), Ohio Batch 514081 Sheet 773. Surname is incorrectly spelled "Howe".

[280] 1860 federal census, population schedule, Rich Hill, Muskingum County, OH, p. 388 (stamped) p. 111 (written), dwelling #792 and family #792. Even though the 1850 census shows her age 34 and born in North Carolina no other references show a North Carolina birth place. Furthermore, Leon A. Goodale in the reference cited above gives Massachusetts as her birth place which agrees with the birth place given in this 1860 census. That reference does not specify her date of birth but locates her between siblings who were born only 21 months apart, thus the approximate month of Safrona's birth.

[281] Ibid.

[282] Muskingum County, Ohio, Marriages, Book IV 1848-1865 (Zanesville, OH: Muskingum County Chapter, Ohio Genealogical Society, 1983), p. 45.

Safronia's birth date estimate was based on the 1860 census and by "slotting" the date between the specific birth dates of her brothers, James and Austin.

In 1804, when Alfred was born, Thomas Jefferson was the third president of the United States, which had gained independence 28 years previously. Ohio, soon to be Alfred's home, had just begun to function as a state a year earlier.[283] Alfred arrived in Ohio with his parents and siblings by 2 May 1818 when his sister Margaret was born. See his father, Abner's, record for a further description of the estimated time of arrival of the family in Ohio.

Safronia Prouty's immigrant ancestor, Richard Prouty, had arrived in Scituate, Massachusetts, before 1676 when he fought in King Phillips War.[284] She was the sixth generation of Proutys in America. Safronia's Goodale immigrant ancestor, Robert Goodale, had arrived in Salem, Massachusetts from England by 1636.[285] Her mother was the sixth generation of Goodales in America. Other New England direct ancestors include: Abraham Temple who died after 1639 in Massachusetts; Abraham How who died before 2 November 1676 in Boston; Richard Temple who died 15 Mar 1689 in Concord, Massachusetts; Catherine Kilham who died 1645/1646 in Salem, Massachusetts; Abraham Howe who died 21 November 1683 in Roxbury, Massachusetts; Lt. James Torrey who died 6 July 1665 Scituate, Massachusetts; Deborah Hadlocke who died 28 January 1743; Joseph House who died 24 February 1757 in Lancaster, Massachusetts; Eunice Marshall who died 17 January 1831, West Bolyston, Massachusetts; Prudence Wilder who died 11 June 1842, West Bolyston, Massachusetts.

---

[283] In 1953 President Eisenhower signed an act with retroactive effect which admitted Ohio to the Union on March 1, 1803.

[284] Charles Henry Pope, Prouty (Proute) Genealogy (Boston, MA: author, 1910).

[285] George E. Williams, Descendants of Robert Goodale/Goodell, p. 5.

According to Goodale, the Proutys moved west [Ohio] in 1814.[286] Robertson comments on the schools in Bristol Township during this period:

> One of the first schools in Bristol was taught by a Yankee by the name of Samuel Shattuck, etc....[287]

The spelling of "Safronia" took many forms on various documents. Examples are: Frona, Sophroanya, Sophronia, Sophronya, Sephranya, Saphronia, and Safroaney.[288] It is not known where she is buried.

When Alfred was nine years old, two events occurred which impacted greatly the future safety of his family to settle in Ohio. On 10 September 1813 the British were defeated in the Battle of Lake Erie by the United States naval forces under the command of Oliver Hazard Perry. This defeat quickly led to the cessation of British encouragement of the Indians to attack the Ohio settlers. Less than a month later, 5 October 1813, Tecumseh lay dead from wounds inflicted during his last battle.[289] He was a warrior and a mystical prophet who had spent many years trying to forge an alliance of all the Indian tribes of North America to resist the incursion of settlers onto their native lands.

We do not know how Alfred and his parents and siblings travelled from Virginia to Muskingum County. A typical overland route at that time would have been over the National Road from Cumberland, Maryland to Wheeling (which was completed in 1818) and over Zane's Trace from Wheeling to Muskingum County. This trace is

---

[286] Leon A. Goodale, Notes on the Lives of Edward and Sarah Temple Goodale, p. 32.

[287] Charles Robertson, History of Morgan County, Ohio (Chicago: L. H. Watkins & Co., 1886), p. 481.

[288] Muskingum County, OH, Deed Bks S:349, U:666.

[289] Allan W. Eckert, The Frontiersmen, A Narrative (Boston: Little, Brown, & Co., 1967), p. 584.

described in more detail in Alfred's father's portion of this genealogy).
Likewise, it is not known how Safronia and her parents and siblings
travelled from Massachusetts.

March 1828, at the age of 24 and two years before his marriage,
Alfred bought land for the first time when he purchased 81 acres
from John Addy, (R11 T13 S26).[290] This land, the southern half of
the pioneer farm owned by his father, was briefly owned by John
Addy. Six years later, Alfred bought 80 acres in Meigs Township
about 5 miles south of the first property.[291] This property was sold
about four years later,[292] and it is most likely that the family never
took up residence there. Alfred still held title to the original property
in 1890, but it had been sold by the time of his death in 1900.

Alfred apparently spent his entire adult life in Rich Hill Township; all
census records show him there. His first appearance on a census was
in 1830 where he is listed as head of household.[293] He is listed on
all subsequent extant censuses through 1900. He last appeared on the
1900 census and is shown living with his son Henry Landon, so it can
be concluded that since his headstone shows his death in 1900 he must
have died between June 1900 and the end of that year.

Alfred must have been a vigorous man. He had eight children by
Safronia and then had three more by Rachel. The last child was born
when Alfred was 63 years old. He was 96 years old when he died.
He was a man with little formal education and the 1900 census reveals
that he could neither read or write. He signed documents with an X.

As a consequence of Alfred's longevity and the long life of one of his
grandsons, Ira Teters Howell, we, as late as 1990, are allowed to

[290] Muskingum County, OH, Deed Bk, I:625.

[291] Muskingum County, OH, Deed Bk, S:398.

[292] Muskingum County, OH, Deed Bk, U:666.

[293] 1830 federal census, population schedule, Rich Hill Township, Muskingum
County, OH, p. 261.

"reach back" nearly two centuries. When interviewed in 1990, Ira, who was 101 years old, recalled when his grandfather, Alfred, died. He said that Alfred died on the front porch of his home and Ira was sent to the nearest neighbor to summon aid. In Alfred's lifetime our nation fought four wars: War of 1812, Mexican War, Civil War, and the Spanish American War. The state of Ohio , which at the time of his birth was still experiencing Indian raids, had at the time of his death become a populous industrial and agricultural state. Furthermore during that time Ohio had produced five presidents of the United States.

Known children of Alfred and Safronia, all of whom were born on the farm near Spratt in Rich Hill Township in Muskingum County, include:

74   i.   Thomas William[5] Howell, born 1831/1833; married 16 September 1857 in Muskingum County, Amanda Bryant.[294]

75   ii.   Sarah Ann Howell, born 1834; married 17 July 1853 in Muskingum County, Reason Riggs.[295]

76   iii. James Wesley Howell, born 1835/36; married 27 June 1854 in Muskingum County, Jane Elliott.[296]

+77   iv. George Howell, born 1837/1839; died August 1876 in Iowa; married 9 May 1863 in Muskingum County, Jane Lyons.[297]

---

[294] Muskingum County, Ohio, Marriages, 1848-1865, Book 4, p. 45.

[295] Ibid., p. 148.

[296] Ibid., p. 130.

[297] No official record found. The year of the marriage is verified by Jane's obituary; and the month, day, and year are found on a page (a xerox copy of which is in the hands of Robert W. Cameron [1993]) in the family bible of John Jordan and Jane Young. Copyright 1896.

78   v.   Mary Ann Howell, born 1842/1843.

79   vi.   Alfred Howell, born 1845/1846.

80   vii.   John F. Howell, born 1847/1848; married 21 January 1868 in Muskingum County, Mary E. Morrison.[298]

Even though the 1870 census[299] shows a 16-year old male, Ira M. Howell, in the dwelling, it is likely that he is not a son since he does not appear on the 1860 census cited above.

Known children of Alfred and Rachel, all of whom were born on the farm near Spratt in Rich Hill Township in Muskingum County, include:

81   i.   Marion Cook[5] Howell, born 12 June 1862; died 23 February 1947 in Rich Hill Township, Muskingum County; married 30 November 1881, Nancy Ellen Anderson.[300]

82   ii.   Thomas Frank Howell, born 12 January 1865; died 25 February 1913; married 7 March 1886 in Muskingum County, Florence C. Humphrey.[301]

---

[298] Muskingum County Marriages, 1865-1869, Book V, (Zanesville, OH: Muskingum County Genealogical Society, n.d.), p. 14.

[299] 1870 federal census, population schedule, Rich Hill Township, Muskingum County, OH, p. 309, dwelling #163, family #166.

[300] No official record found. However, a letter from his grandson Raymond Moore Howell dated 18 February 1990 provides the data. Muskingum County Cemetery Book, Meigs & Rich Hill Townships, Muskingum County Genealogical Society, 1981, page 4 of Rich Hill Township section, verifies the year of death 1947.

[301] Muskingum County Marriage Records, Marriage Book 10, 1885-1889 (Zanesville, OH: Muskingum County Genealogical Society, n.d.), p. 96.

83   iii.   Henry Landon Howell, born 21 September 1867;
                     died 13 December 1963 in Zanesville, Muskingum
                     County; married 1891/1892, Sarah Alice Johnson.

38. Martha[4] Howell (Abner[3], William[2], Hugh[1]) was born 10 March
1807[302] in Virginia, probably in Loudoun County,[303] and died 20
September 1879. She is buried in Carr's Methodist Church Cemetery,
near Norwich, Union Township, Muskingum Co., Ohio.[304]   She
married 17 September 1825[305] in Muskingum County, Ohio, John
Shamblin, who was born 18 August 1771 in Loudoun County,
Virginia[306] and died 18 March 1864 in Muskingum County, Ohio.
She married, second 14 November 1864, Richard H. Hogan, born 16
January 1790 and died 27 January 1874 and buried in same cemetery
with wife and her first husband. She is named as an heir of Abner
Howell, along with Abner, Jr., and John Howell, in deed to George
Howell, 15 January 1845, (R11 T13 S26).[307]

---

[302] Family bible record of Abner Howell, Jr.

[303] For description of the speculation of place of birth see Generation Three,
Abner Howell.

[304] Cemetery Inscriptions of Perry and Washington Townships of Muskingum
County, Ohio (Zanesville, OH: Muskingum County Genealogical Society, 1986), p.
25.

[305] Muskingum County, Ohio, Marriages, 1818-1835, **Book 2** (Zanesville, OH:
Muskingum County Genealogical Society, 1977), p. 218.

[306] 1850 federal census, population schedule, Perry Township, Muskingum
County, OH, p. 480, dwelling #104, family #104. Also DAR application of Jessie
Claire Tomlinson.

[307] Muskingum County, OH, Deed Bk 10:15.

The 1850 census[308] shows her as a 42 year- old Virginia native living with her 70-year old husband, John Shamblin, and six children. The 1860 census[309] shows her as a 50-year old Virginia native living with her 85-year old husband.

Children of John and Martha, all born in Ohio, include:[310]

84   i.   Martha Priscilla[5] Shamblin, born 3 January 1828; died 1 August 1858 in Muskingum County; married 21 July 1847, John Wesley Tomlinson.[311]

85   ii.   Alfred Shamblin, born 1827/1828; married 25 November 1852, Sarah E. Howell. Enlisted as private, 8 October 1862 in Company E, 2nd Regiment of Ohio Volunteer Infantry. Died of pneumonia 21 February 1863 at Stone River, Murfreesboro, Tennessee.[312]

86   iii. Aaron Shamblin, born 1830; married 25 December 1857 in Muskingum County, Margaret Ann Cherry.[313]

87   iv.   French Shamblin, born 1832.

---

[308] 1850 federal census, population schedule, Muskingum County, Perry Township, OH, p. 480, dwelling #104, family #104.

[309] 1860 federal census, population schedule, Muskingum County, Perry Township, OH, p. 135, dwelling #98, family #98.

[310] Birth dates estimated from 1850 census except as otherwise noted.

[311] DAR application of Jessie Claire Tomlinson.

[312] Official Roster of the Soldiers of the State of Ohio in the War of the Rebellion, 1861-1866, vol. II (Cincinnati, OH: Willstock Baldwin & Co., 1886), pp. 47, 730.

[313] Muskingum County, Ohio, Marriages, 1848-1865, Book IV, p. 81.

88   v.   Mary Ann Shamblin, born 28 November 1838; married 11 August 1859 in Zanesville, Muskingum County, Richard H. Bowman.[314]

89   vi.   Frances Shamblin, born 1841; married 17 June 1858 in Muskingum County, Henry D. Richcreek.[315]

39.   Elizabeth[4] Howell (Abner[3], William[2], Hugh[1]) was born 10 December 1808 probably in Loudoun County, Virginia.[316] We know very little beyond her birth date.

After her father's death, her name was mentioned in a petition to sell land that had belonged to him.[317] Her name was given as Elizabeth Howell, so she had not married as of 1847. This is the last record we have been able to find for her.

Abner's daughter should not be confused with another Elizabeth Howell, who has been found in the same period in Muskingum County. The other Elizabeth married a Joseph Crumbaker 12 August 1845,[318] and was listed in the will of her father, Phillip Howell.[319] This branch of the Howell family came from Allegheny County, Pennsylvania. A relationship between them and the Loudoun County Howells has not been established, if one ever existed.

---

[314]Ibid., p. 183.

[315]Ibid., p. 183.

[316] Family Bible Records of Abner Howell, Jr.

[317] Muskingum County, OH, Appointment Docket S, 1846-1848, p. 400.

[318] Muskingum County, Ohio, Marriages, Book 3, 1835-1848.

[319] Guernsey County, OH, Will Bk I:373.

40.   Amanda[4] Howell (Abner[3], William[2], Hugh[1]) was born 29 June 1810[320] in Virginia, probably in Loudoun County[321], and died after June 1850[322]. She married 16 May 1831[323] in Muskingum County, Ohio, Alexander Grandstaff, who was born about 1806 in Ohio County, Virginia[324] and died during the period 1850 to 1913. He was the son of Lewis and Esther Grandstaff.[325] Lewis Grandstaff's earliest known ancestor was Dietrich (Cranzdorf) Krantzdorf who was born before 1650 and died before 1714. They came from Hornback, Germany in the Palatinate area.

The 1840 census shows Alex Grandstaff as head of a family with the following data:[326]

Table 2. Alexander Grandstaff Household in 1840

Sex	<5	5-9	10-14	30-39
Males	1		1	1
Females	1	3		1

---

[320] Family Bible Records of Abner Howell, Jr.

[321] For description of the speculation of place of birth see Generation Three, Abner Howell.

[322] 1850 federal census, population schedule, Benton Township, Hocking County, OH, p. 437, dwelling #190, family #192.

[323] Muskingum County, Ohio, Marriages, 1818-1835, Book 2, p. 218.

[324] Doris J. Brown & Margaret Stainbrook, Grandstaff/Grindstaff Family (Pittsburg, PA: Press Graphics, n.d.), pp. 293-294.

[325] Ibid.

[326] 1840 federal census, population schedule, Rich Hill Township, Muskingum County, OH, p. 482.

It is noted that the one male of age 10 through 14 would have been born before Amanda and Alexander were married; so he may not be a son of theirs. It is also noted that only two of the three females aged 5 through 9 appear in the list of children, i.e., Mary and Mia Alice. If the third female was one of their children she may have died or left the home by 1850.

By 1850 Amanda is found in Benton Township of Hocking County, Ohio, with her husband, who was a shoemaker, and eight children, all of whom were born in Ohio. Since Eleanor J. was not listed she apparently died earlier that year.[327]

Since her daughter, Martha Ann, was married in Hocking County, 4 October 1860, it is likely that the family still lived in the area at that time.

Alexander Grandstaff and wife, Amanda, were grantors in a quitclaim[328] to George Howell, 27 Apr 1847 for 163.26 acres (R11 T13 S26) in Rich Hill Township of Muskingum County, Ohio, thus proving her as a daughter of Abner Howell.

Children of Alexander and Amanda, all born in Ohio, include:[329]

90   i.   Mary[5] Grandstaff, born about 1833; married 13 March 1853 in Vinton County, Ohio, Samuel Saler.

91   ii.   Martha Ann Grandstaff, born about 1835; married 4 October 1860 in Hocking County, Ohio, Peter Ebert.

92   iii.   Joseph Grandstaff, born about 1837.

---

[327] Brown & Stainbrook, Grandstaff/Grindstaff Family, p. 293.

[328] Muskingum County, OH, Deed Bk, 13:7.

[329] Brown & Stainbrook, Grandstaff/Grindstaff Family, pp. 293, 294.

93	iv.	Mia Alice Grandstaff, born about 1839.
94	v.	Julian Grandstaff, born about 1841.
95	vi.	John Grandstaff, born about 1845; married Louisa Hyatt 14 August 1864.
96	vii.	Hanna F. Grandstaff, born about 1847.
97	viii.	Eleanor J. Grandstaff, born 1847; died 1850.
98	ix.	Amanda Grandstaff, born about 1849.
99	x.	Alexander Grandstaff, Jr., born about 1850.

41.   Frances/Fanny Howell was born 2 October 1812, probably in Loudoun County, Virginia.[330] She married Samuel Pyle 1 May 1828 in Muskingum County, Ohio.[331]

Fanny and Samuel were among other heirs, who signed over Abner's land to Alfred Howell 15 March 1844.[332] Both of them signed their names in cursive, showing that they could read and write.

The Pyles were found in the 1850 Ohio census. At that time they and Fanny's brother, George, were living in Vinton County, Ohio - Swan Township.[333] In the census their surname was recorded as "Piles." Also from this record we learn that Samuel was born in Pennsylvania about 1790 (age 59). Frances A. (as recorded) is shown as age 38 with a birthplace of Virginia.

---

[330] Family Bible Records of Abner Howell, Jr.

[331] Muskingum County, Ohio, Marriages, 1818-1835, Book 2, **p. 218.**

[332] Muskingum County, OH, Deed Bk 18:453.

[333] 1850 federal census, population schedule, Swan Township, Vinton County, OH, p. 654, dwelling #150, family #151.

The probable children of Samuel and Frances Pyle were identified in the 1850 census, as follows:

100   i.   William Pyle, born about 1830 in Ohio.

101   ii.   Isac (?) Pyle, born about 1833 in Ohio.

102   iii. Samuel Pyle, born about 1834 in Ohio.

We tried to find the Pyles in the 1860 Ohio census. A number of Pyles were found but the ages and other data did not fit our couple. They could have died between census years, or they could have moved farther west into another state.

42. Eaura/Ura[4] Howell (Abner[3], William[2], Hugh[1]) was born 9 August 1813, probably in Loudoun County, Virginia.[334] She married a William Hyde 26 September 1833, in Muskingum County, Ohio.[335] Her given name on this document is shown as "Urey."

After her father's death, Ura and William Hyde joined other relatives in signing over 163.26 acres of land to Ura's brother, Alfred Howell.[336] The quitclaim, dated 15 March 1844, reflects William Hyde's written signature. Ura signed by mark.

An effort was made to learn more about the Hydes by locating them in the 1850 Ohio census. This search was not successful. A number of William Hydes were found in the 1850 Ohio Census Index, but when the actual microfilm records were checked, it became apparent that the Williams found were not the right ones. They were either too old or way too young. In addition to Muskingum County, the counties

---

[334] Family Bible Records of Abner Howell, Jr.

[335] <u>Muskingum County Ohio, Marriage Book 2</u>, p. 218.

[336] Muskingum County, OH, Deed Bk 18:453.

surrounding it were also checked. As a result of these negative searches, we don't know if the Hydes had children or not.

43. Mary Ann[4] Howell (Abner[3], William[2], Hugh[1]) was born 20 October 1815 probably in Loudoun County, Virginia.[337] She married George Holmes 8 March 1838, in Muskingum County, Ohio.[338]

After her father's death, Mary and George Holmes were involved in the transactions to dispose of Abner's estate. On 15 March 1844, George and Mary Ann Holmes (along with other siblings) quitclaimed to Alfred Howell 163.26 acres of land.[339] In a petition to sell land filed 17 April 1847, George Holmes is mentioned as the administrator of the estate of Abner Howell, deceased.[340] This document also refers to Mary Ann, his wife.

On 2 August 1850, we find George and Mary Ann Holmes, age 46 and 34, respectively, living in Muskingum County, Hopewell Township.[341] Birthplaces for both were given as Virginia. George's occupation was given as farmer. Mary Ann could not read or write. Living with them was a 12-year old girl named Elizabeth Redman, relationship unknown. She was born in Ohio.

In 1860, George and Mary Holmes were still living in Hopewell Township, but George was now a carpenter.[342] At this time, they

---

[337] Family Bible Records of Abner Howell, Jr.

[338] Muskingum County Ohio, Marriage Book #3, 1835-1848, p. 107.

[339] Muskingum County, OH, Deed Bk 18:453.

[340] Muskingum County, OH, Appointment Docket S (1846-1848), p. 400.

[341] 1850 federal census, population schedule, Hopewell Township, Muskingum County, OH, p. 88, dwelling #289, family #290.

[342] 1860 federal census, population schedule, Hopewell Township, Muskingum County, OH, p. 98, dwelling #128, family #126.

apparently owned no real estate, but did own personal property valued at $75. The census shows no children living in this family. It is quite likely that this couple did not have any children of their own, or none that survived beyond childhood.

44. George Joseph[4] Howell (Abner[3], William[2], Hugh[1]) was born 8 September 1817,[343] either in Loudoun County, Virginia or Muskingum County, Ohio.[344] He died 19 July 1886 in Flag Springs, Andrew County, Missouri.[345] He married Martha Eady or Eddy, 9 January 1840 in Muskingum County, Ohio.[346] She was born 20 October 1818 in Muskingum County and died 12 May 1899 in Flag Springs.[347] Both George and Martha are buried in the Flag Springs Cemetery.[348]

George first set up housekeeping in 1840 near his father and older brother, Alfred.[349] The next year his father died intestate, but a series of quitclaims and deeds showed a division of Abner's property among 13 legal heirs.[350] John and Abner Howell, together with

---

[343] Family Bible Records of Abner Howell, Jr.

[344] The only record of George's birth place comes form census records and they are divided. The 1850 census and the 1880 census of son, James, say VA; the 1860, 1870 and 1880 census say OH. Complete citations follow.

[345] Flag Springs Cemetery Inscriptions, Vol. IV (Savannah, MO: Andrew County Historical Society, 1977), p. 32.

[346] Muskingum County, Ohio Marriage Book #3, 1835-1848, p. 15.

[347] Flag Springs Cemetery, p. 32. Also Dorothy J. McMackin, comp. Newspaper Gleanings of Andrew County and Surrounding Area (Stayton, OR: Jordan Valley Heritage House, 1986), p. 508.

[348] Flag Springs Cemetery, p. 32.

[349] 1840 federal census, population schedule, Rich Hill Township, Muskingum County, OH, p. 485.

[350] Muskingum County, OH, Deed Bks 18:453, 10:15, 13:5-7.

John and Martha Shamlin assigned their claim to George on 18 January 1845 for $225.[351]　George was named in three additional quitclaim documents in 1847 and 1848: Alfred and Sophrona Howell to George Howell; George and Martha Howell to William Cariens; Alexander and Amanda Grandstaff to George Howell.[352]　On 18 January 1845 he purchased 80 acres in Hocking County from Joseph Kaler,[353] where the family remained for the next 19 years.　By 1850, the portion of Hocking County where they lived became Swan Township, Vinton County and George and Martha were found, now with a family of 6 children ranging in age from less than a year to 9 years of age.[354]　One household away, George's sister, Frances (Fanny) Pyle was living with her husband, Samuel and three teen-age children.[355]　Both George and Samuel were listed as farmers.　Not far away in Benton Township, Hocking County, George's sister, Amanda Grandstaff lived with her family of eight children.[356]　Two more children were born to George and Martha between 1850 and 1860,[357] but by 1863, they sold their Vinton County property and were on the move again.[358]

George and his family found their way to Andrew County, Missouri not far from St. Joseph and fairly close to the Kansas border.　They

---

[351] Muskingum County, OH, Deed Bk 10:14.

[352] Muskingum County, OH, Deed Bks 13:5, 13:6, and 13:7.

[353] Hocking County, OH, Deed Bk I:324.

[354] 1850 federal census, population schedule, Swan Township, Vinton County, OH, p. 654, dwelling #152, family #153.

[355] Ibid., p. 654, dwelling #150, family #151.

[356] 1850 federal census, population schedule, Benton Township, Hocking County, OH, p. 437, dwelling #190, family #192.

[357] 1860 federal census, population schedule, Swan Township, Vinton County, OH, p. 294, dwelling #441, family #333.

[358] Vinton County, OH, Deed Bk 9:319.

A portion of Empire Township, Andrew County, Missouri showing
"G. Howell" and "J. Howell" in section 22 along the Platte
River.

George Howell's grave marker at Flag Springs, Andrew County, Missouri is substantial and well kept.

settled first in Platte Township in the northeast corner of the county and were found there in the 1870 census.[359]   Interestingly, as head of household he is listed as Joseph (middle name), age 52, with wife, Martha, and five of their eight children still living with them. Living next door was newly married son, James, his wife, Mary and a daughter, Ellen, 2 months old.[360]   Not far away, was the Joseph Lanning family,[361] whose daughter, Mary, had just married James. Mary had at least 11 brothers and sisters and was probably the oldest. By 1880, George and Martha, age 65 and 64, were found in Empire Township, Andrew County. Still listed as living with them were Mary Ann, Alfred, Ambrose and Emily.[362]   However, Ambrose, Alfred and sister, Eliza J. had already or were soon to set up their own household nearby, for Ambrose and Alfred were counted twice that year![363]   Also nearby were newly married son, John W. and wife, Lucinda (Turpin),[364] the Joseph Lanning family,[365] and the Edmond Brooke family (George's daughter, Sarah).[366]

George died 19 July 1886, leaving personal property valued at $536 and property consisting of an 186 acre homestead and two 12 acre

---

[359] 1870 federal census, population schedule, Platte Township, Andrew County, MO, p. 62, dwelling #433, family #435.

[360] Ibid., p. 62, dwelling #434, family #436.

[361] 1870 federal census, population schedule, Platte Township, Andrew County, MO, p. 19, dwelling #129, family #131.

[362] 1880 federal census, population schedule, Empire Township, Andrew County, MO, p. 9, dwelling #73, family #75.

[363] 1880 federal census, population schedule, Empire Township, Andrew County, MO, p. 8, dwelling #58, family #60.

[364] 1880 federal census, population schedule, Subdistrict 44, Andrew County, MO, p. 2, dwelling #13, family #15.

[365] Ibid., p. 3, dwelling #26, family #28.

[366] 1880 federal census, population schedule, Platte Township, Andrew County, MO, p. 11, dwelling (not given), family #99.

plots.[367] His wife, Martha, as administrix, presented an inventory of his estate on 15 October 1886. Interestingly, his probate records also contained an undated letter signed by son, James Howell, asking his mother not be appointed administrix because she was old, infirm and unable to transact the business required. A Public Administrator was requested in her stead. Named also in the letter were heirs Sarah A. Brooke, Emily Wilson and John W. Howell as supporting this request. Nothing in the papers suggest this request was acted upon by the Court.[368]

Known children of George and Martha (Eady/Eddy) Howell include:

103   i.   Mary Ann[5] Howell, born December 1840,[369] probably in Muskingum County, Ohio.[370] She died, unmarried, 18 March 1882 and is buried in the Flag Springs Cemetery, Andrew County, Missouri.[371]

104   ii.   Eliza Jane Howell, born 22 May 1842,[372] probably in Muskingum County, Ohio.[373] She died 9 November 1897 and is buried in the Flag Springs Cemetery.[374]   She married Burrows

---

[367] Andrew County, MO, Probate Record #1420.

[368] Ibid.

[369] Flag Springs Cemetery, p. 32.

[370] Muskingum County is assumed because purchase of property in Vinton County was in 1845 and brother, James, was born in Muskingum County in 1844.

[371] Flag Springs Cemetery, p. 32.

[372] Flag Springs Cemetery, p. 35.

[373] Muskingum County is assumed because purchase of property in Vinton County was in 1845 and brother, James was born in Muskingum County in 1844.

[374] Flag Springs Cemetery, p. 35.

Powell, born about 1862/1863 probably in Missouri.[375] They had at least three children, Nettie M., Charles S. Burrows and one other son.[376]

+105   iii.   James A. Howell, born 25 September 1844,[377] Zanesville, Muskingum County, Ohio.

106   iv.   Sarah A. Howell, born October 1846, Hocking County, Ohio.[378] She died in 1925 and is buried in Flag Springs Cemetery.[379] She married, 22 September 1867,[380] Edmond Cone Brooke, born December 1847, Ohio. He died 7 March 1934 and is also buried in Flag Springs Cemetery.[381] They had 11 children: James Edmond, Martha J., Alva L., George F., Mattie A., Laura S., Dora M. or W., Lelia J. or Lilly B., Archbald H. and Arthur C. (twins), and Daisy E. Brooke.[382]

---

[375] Assumed from census ages of children.

[376] 1870 federal census, population schedule, Whitesville Township, Andrew County, MO, p. 13, dwelling #88, family #90. Also McMackin, Newspaper Gleanings, p. 463.

[377] James A. Howell Civil War Pension File #1066225, National Archives and Records Service, Washington, D.C.

[378] Flag Springs Cemetery, p. 29.

[379] Ibid.

[380] Andrew County, MO, Marriage Record Book A:412, #2342.

[381] Flag Springs Cemetery, p. 29.

[382] 1880 federal census, population schedule, Platte Township, Andrew County, MO, p. 11, dwelling (not given), family #88. Also Edmond C. Brooke will, Andrew County Probate Record #4086. Flag Springs Cemetery, p. 29.

107   v.   John W. Howell, born 1847, Hocking County,
                  Ohio. He died in 1925 in King City, Gentry
                  County, Missouri.[383] He married, 6 November
                  1879, Linda Turpin.[384] She was born 1851 in
                  Kentucky, died in 1928. Both are buried in the
                  King City Cemetery.[385]   They had 1 child,
                  Norman A. Howell.[386]

108   vi.   Alfred Howell, born 12 April 1850, Vinton
                  County, Ohio, died 17 February 1936 and is buried
                  in Flag Springs Cemetery.[387] He was a member
                  of the Methodist Episcopal Church in Union Star;
                  never married, was living with his brother,
                  Ambrose in 1880.[388]

109   vii.   Ambrose Howell, born 5 March 1852, Vinton
                  County, Ohio, died 24 May 1937.[389] He married
                  19 September 1883 in King City, Gentry County,
                  Missouri, Elizabeth Booth.[390] She was born 20
                  March 1853 in Waukesha County, Wisconsin and

---

[383] King City Missouri Cemetery (St. Joseph, MO: Northwest Missouri
Genealogical Society, 1982), p. 10.

[384] Andrew County, MO, Marriage Record Bk B:184.

[385] King City Cemetery, p. 11.

[386] Flag Springs Cemetery, p. 32.

[387] Savannah Reporter (Savannah, Andrew Co., MO) 28 February 1936, p. 5
(obituary).

[388] 1880 federal census, population schedule, Empire Township, Andrew County,
MO, p. 8, dwelling #58, family #60.

[389] Andrew County, MO, Probate Record #4246; also Savannah Reporter
(Savannah, Andrew Co., MO) 4 June 1937, p. 5.

[390] Andrew County, MO, Marriage Record Bk 1:145.

died 18 November 1934.[391] Both Ambrose and Elizabeth are buried in Flag Springs Cemetery. They had at least 4 children: Mabel, Wallace, Walter E., Orville E. Howell.[392]

110   viii.   Emma/Emily Howell, born March 1855, Vinton County, Ohio.[393] She married 20 September 1883, Joseph S. Wilson.[394] He was born 11 March 1857, died 2 February 1945 and is buried in Whitesville Cemetery, Whitesville, Andrews County, Missouri.[395]

45. Margaret[4] Howell (Abner[3], William[2], Hugh[1]) was born 2 May 1818[396] in Rix Mill,[397] Rich Hill Township,[398] Muskingum County, Ohio. Margaret died of influenza in Rix Mill, Muskingum County, 28 February 1905,[399] and was buried in Rich Hill Cemetery,

---

[391] Flag Springs Cemetery, p. 32.

[392] 1900 federal census, population schedule, Empire Township, Andrew County, MO, dwelling #165, family #173, ED 4, sheet A9.

[393] Ibid., dwelling #206, family #217, ED 4, sheet A11.

[394] Andrew County, MO, Marriage Record Bk 1:144.

[395] Cemetery Inscriptions, Book IV (Savannah, MO: Andrew County Historical Society, 1977), (Whitesville Cemetery), p. 77.

[396] Family Bible Records of Abner Howell, Jr.

[397] Muskingum County, OH, Court of Common Pleas, Probate Division, Death Certificate, vol. 4, p. 121.

[398] Zanesville Signal (Zanesville, Muskingum Co., OH), 1 Mar 1905, p. 3, column 5; Zanesville Daily Times Recorder (Zanesville, Muskingum Co., OH), 1 March 1905, p. 5, column 5.

[399] Death Certificate of Margaret Lyons cited above.

Muskingum County.[400]   She married Robert Lyons[401] 9 April
1840[402] in Muskingum County. He was born 22 March 1819[403] in
Washington County, Pennsylvania, the son of John and Elizabeth
(McCormick) Lyons. Robert died in Rich Hill Township 5 November
1908, and is buried beside Margaret.[404]

Margaret Lyons is one of 10 grantors in a quitclaim to Alfred Howell,
15 March 1844 to the family farm in Rich Hill.[405] She appears, with
her husband, in the 1850, 1860, 1870, 1880, and 1900 censuses of
Rich Hill Township, Muskingum County, Ohio.[406] She lived in Rich
Hill Township all her life.[407]

From the history cited above it is recorded that she and Robert
recalled many of the early events of this part of the state. They
remembered the arrival of the first steamboat to the Zanesville port

---

[400] Obituary of Margaret Lyons cited above. Also Muskingum County Cemetery
Book - Rich Hill Township (Zanesville, OH: Muskingum County Genealogical
Society, 1981), p. 20 of Rich Hill Township section.

[401] J. Hope Sutor, Past and Present of Zanesville and Muskingum County, Ohio
(Chicago; S.J. Clarke Publishing Co., 1905), p. 707.

[402] Zanesville Daily Times Recorder (Zanesville, Muskingum Co., OH), 1 March
1905, p. 5, column 5. Year of marriage verified by J. Hope Sutor, p. 707.

[403] Muskingum County, OH, Court of Common Pleas, Probate Division, Death
Certificate, vol. IV, p. 123.

[404] Death Certificate of Robert Lyons cited above.

[405] Muskingum County, OH, Deed Bk, 18:453.

[406] 1850 federal census, population schedule, Rich Hill Township, Muskingum
County, OH, p. 480, dwelling #135, family #135; 1860, ibid., p. 383, dwelling #719,
family #719; 1870, ibid., p. 304, dwelling #92, family #95; 1880, ibid., Village of
Rix Mills, p. 274, dwelling #4, family #4; 1900, ibid., Chandlersville, p. 223B,
dwelling #228, family #234.

[407] Zanesville Signal, 1 March 1905, p. 3, column 5.

and building of the old Y bridge. They owned large tracts of land in Rich Hill Township, and still held valuable realty in 1908. By that time they had retired to a fine home in Rixville. Robert had set up additionally, saw mills for Blandy Company of Zanesville and operated one himself.

The children of Margaret and Robert (all of which were born in Rich Hill Township), were:[408]

111   i.   John[5] Lyons, born April 1841; died 5 May 1916 in Rich Hill.[409] He married 2 January 1866 in Muskingum County, Hannah Margaret Brown. He was a Civil War veteran having served as a private in Company C, 159 Ohio Infantry from 2 May 1864 to 23 August 1864.[410]

112   ii.   Elizabeth Lyons, born February 1843; died 1932.[411] She married 12 February 1868 in Muskingum County, Philip Leedom.[412]

113   iii.   William Lyons, born 25 April 1844; died 1905/1933. He married 5 September 1867 in Muskingum County, Nancy Blackstone. He was a veteran of the Civil War having served from 2

---

[408] J. Hope Sutor, <u>Past & Present of City of Zanesville & Muskingum County, Ohio</u>, p. 707.

[409] Ohio State Death Certificate #33910, on file at Ohio Historical Society in Columbus, OH.

[410] <u>Official Roster of the Soldiers of the State of Ohio in the War of the Rebellion</u>, Vol. IX (n.p.: Ohio Valley Press, 1889), p. 285.

[411] <u>Muskingum County Cemetery Book</u>, p. 26 of Rich Hill Township section.

[412] <u>Muskingum County, Ohio Marriages Book V, 1865-1869</u>, p. 52.

May 1864 to 23 August 1864, 160th Regiment of Ohio National Guard.[413]

114   iv.   Andrew Lyons, born August 1845; died 1927.[414] He married 2 September 1869 in Guernsey County, Evaline M. Dennis.[415]

115   v.   Jane Lyons, born 23 February 1847; died 19 November 1933 in Lamont, Grant County, Oklahoma.[416] She married, (1) 9 May 1863 in Muskingum County George Howell, son of Alfred[4] Howell (Abner[3], William[2], Hugh[1]). George Howell was born 1837/1839 near Spratt, Rich Hill Township and died in August 1876 in Iowa. She married, (2) John Jordan Young, born 26 March 1829 in England and died 31 January 1924 in Lamont, Grant County, Oklahoma.[417]

116   vi.   James Lyons, born 1848; died 1890.[418]

117   vii.   Lucinda Lyons, 1850/1851; died after November 1933.

118   viii. Joshua Lyons, born 11 August 1852; died 8 March 1941 in Columbus, Franklin County, Ohio. He

---

[413] Official Roster of the Soldiers of the State of Ohio, IX (N.p.: The Ohio Valley Press, 1889), p. 285.

[414] Muskingum County Cemetery Book, p. 21 of Rich Hill Township section.

[415] International Genealogical Index, (IGI), LDS, Ohio.

[416] Death Certificate, Oklahoma State Board of Health Bureau of Vital Statistics, Registration District 27253, Register No. 27-9.

[417] Ibid.

[418] Muskingum County Cemetery Book, p. 26 of Rich Hill Township section.

was buried at Salt Creek United Presbyterian Church Cemetery, Rich Hill Township. He married 7 May 1878 in Rich Hill Township, Nancy E. Paisley, daughter of John and Martha (Collens) Paisley. She was born 25 October 1852 in Ohio and died 29 September 1832 in Rix Mills, Muskingum County.

46. John[4] Howell (Abner[3], William[2], Hugh[1]), was born 9 March 1820, in Muskingum County, Ohio.[419] He may be the John who married a Lavina Spurgeon 10 November 1835 in Muskingum County, Ohio.[420] He would have been a little young - only 15 years old at the time. In any event, he was out of his father's household by 1840. Only two young males were enumerated in Abner's household that year.[421] One was in age category 10-15 (Madison) and the other was in the 15-20 bracket (Abner, Jr.).

In January 1845, John Howell, with others, signed over his "right, title, interest, claim and demands..." to 163.26 acres of Abner's land to George Howell.[422] This is the last record we have been able to find with John Howell's name on it.

47. Abner[4] Howell, Jr. (Abner[3], William[2], Hugh[1]) was born 11 May 1824[423] on the family farm in Rich Hill Township, Muskingum County, Ohio, died in Knox Township, Guernsey County, Ohio 14 December 1913, and is buried in Hopewell Cemetery of that township.

---

[419] Family Bible Records of Abner Howell, Jr.

[420] Muskingum County, Ohio Marriage Book #3, 1835-1848, p. 15.

[421] 1840 federal census, population schedule, Rich Hill Township, Muskingum County, OH, p. 485.

[422] Muskingum County, OH, Deed Bk 10:14.

[423] Family Bible Records of Abner Howell, Jr.

On 1 May 1845, in Guernsey County, Ohio[424] he married Louisa M. Rolans (Rolens). She was born 3 January 1827 in Knox Township, Guernsey County, and died 2 January 1898 in the same township.[425] She is buried beside her husband. Her parents are unknown.

The above cited Howell Family Bible lists the following children of Abner and Louisa, all of whom were born in Ohio:

119　　　　i.　　　Elizabeth Ann[5] Howell, born 8 April 1846.

120　　　　ii.　　　James Henry Howell, born 6 November 1847.

121　　　　iii.　　　Sarah Jane Howell, born 10 November 1849.

122　　　　iv.　　　Eliza Salena Howell, born 20 October 1851.

123　　　　v.　　　Harriet Elvira Howell, born 11 December 1853.

124　　　　vi.　　　Mary Frances Howell, born, 10 November 1855.

125　　　　vii.　　　Emma Caroline Howell, born 26 November 1857.

126　　　　viii.　　　Louisa Zephaline Howell, born 21 November 1859.

127　　　　ix.　　　Amanda Irvilla Howell, born 9 December 1861.

128　　　　x.　　　William Heslip Howell, born 2 October 1863.

129　　　　xi.　　　Ulysses Preston Howell, born 9 February 1863.

130　　　　xii.　　　Edward Ambrose Howell, born 9 February 1867.

131　　　　xiii.　　　John Franklin Howell, born 4 July 1869.

---

[424] Death Certificate #69234, Ohio Historical Society, Columbus, OH.

[425] Family Bible Records of Abner Howell, Jr.

48.   Madison[4] Howell (Abner[3], William[2], Hugh[1]), was the 13th and last child of Abner and Priscilla (Wade) Howell. He was born on the pioneer farm in Muskingum County, Ohio on 2 September 1826, the date recorded in the Bible record referred to earlier and in the 1900 census.[426]   He died 19 March 1909 in Dade County, Missouri and is buried in the Daughtry Cemetery in that county.   He married Elizabeth, the daughter of Frazier and Annah Storer, natives of Pennsylvania, 27 November 1856, in Muskingum County. Elizabeth was born in January 1832, and she died before her husband, probably 1900-1909, in Dade County, Missouri.   These conclusions about Madison and his wife will be fully documented throughout this section.

Madison was 15 years old when his father died in 1841. After that, he may have gone to live with his brother, Alfred. In any event, he was living with Alfred when the census enumerator came around on 25 September 1850. At the time, he was listed as a 24-year old laborer who could not read or write, in the household of Alfred Howell.[427]

Madison, along with William Howell and James W. Howell (sons of Alfred Howell), purchased land for the first time in 1856. For the sum of $382, they purchased from William J. St. Clair a little over one acre of land in Muskingum County (Part of NE 1/4 of Section 22, Township 13, Range 11).[428]   This property is about a mile north of the farm where Madison was born.

Madison married Elizabeth Storer 27 November 1856, in Muskingum County.[429]   In 1850, the Storer family was living in Guernsey

---

[426] 1900 federal census, population schedule, Dade County, MO, family #13, dwelling #13, ED 71, sheet 1.

[427] 1850 federal census, free schedule, Muskingum County, OH, p. 484, family #194, dwelling #194.

[428] Muskingum County, OH, Deed Bk 31:49.

[429] Muskingum County Ohio Marriages, Book IV, 1848-1865, p. 45.

County, Ohio.[430]   According to information given to the Census, Elizabeth and her parents were born in Pennsylvania. Elizabeth was 19 at the time, suggesting an 1830/1831 date of birth. In 1900, when a specific date of birth was requested, her date of birth was given as January 1832. Earlier census records for Pennsylvania suggest the Storer family was from Allegheny County.

Madison's 1856 marriage date presents a problem because his first child, Chalmers Howard, was born 6 March 1854.[431]   A check of Muskingum County marriage records from 1848-1865 does not reveal an earlier marriage to Elizabeth Storer or any other woman. A check of Guernsey County, Ohio marriage records also does not reveal a marriage record for a Madison Howell between the years 1812-1900.[432]

It is possible that Elizabeth Storer is not Chalmers' mother. However, she is listed as his mother on his 1921 death certificate. Madison is listed as his father on this record. Information for the death record was supplied by Emma Howell, Chalmers' second wife.

Another factor to consider in this marriage date puzzle is information supplied to the census taker in 1900. When asked how long they had been married, Madison and/or Elizabeth answered "48 years." This suggests an 1851/1852 marriage date. It is possible that they did not remember the correct year they married. It is also possible that they went through an earlier marriage ceremony/contract that we have not been able to locate, one that was not recorded by civil authorities. If they knew the correct marriage year, they would have had no reason

---

[430] 1850 census, free schedule, Guernsey County, OH, Adams Township, p. 390, family #132, dwelling #133.

[431] Death Certificate for Chalmers H. Howell, 23 October 1921, Registration District 69, Registered No. 551, Colorado State Department of Health, 4210 E 11th Ave., Denver, CO 90220. Copy in possession of author, Wallace.

[432] Guernsey County, OH, Court of Common Pleas, Court House, Cambridge, OH 43725, to Richard Wallace, 22 October 1991.

to give false information to the census taker. That person would not have known or cared about the accuracy of their answer.

While the original marriage date of Madison and Elizabeth remains in question, there is no question that Chalmers was accepted into the family, along with other family members. He is listed in Madison's household as a 6-year old child in the 1860 Census,[433] and as a 16-year old boy in the 1870 Census.[434] He is pictured in a photograph of Madison Howell's family that was taken by a photographer from Golden City, Missouri, probably in the 1870's.[435]

After their marriage, Madison and Elizabeth remained in Muskingum County until the mid-1860's. Then Madison and his family left Ohio and relocated to Southwest Missouri - Dade County. On 1 April 1867, Elizabeth and Madison Howell sold to Joseph McCune a little over 39 acres of land in Muskingum County located in the following place: NE 1/4 of Section (8), Township (2), Range (5).[436] The price they received for this land was $850. This land was originally purchased for $612 by Elizabeth Howell from George W. Short and his wife, Barbara, on 1 July 1864.[437] This land is found about 14 miles north of the pioneer farm where Madison was born. Contrary to the pioneer farm which was located in the Congress lands (1795-1802), these 39 acres are located in the U.S. Military District.

The above land sale probably signalled the move to Missouri by Madison and his family. By November 1869, the family was living

---

[433] 1860 federal census, free schedule, Muskingum County, OH, p. 111, family #792, dwelling #792.

[434] 1870 federal census, population schedule, Dade County, MO, p. 36, family #21, dwelling #21.

[435] Photograph of the Madison Howell Family in possession of the writer, Wallace.

[436] Muskingum County, OH, Deed Bk 47:536.

[437] Muskingum County, OH, Deed Bk 47:535.

in Dade County, Missouri. On 4 November 1869, Madison and Elizabeth Howell signed a quit claim deed in Dade County, conveying a lot and appurtenances in New Concord, Ohio to Cyrena Storer for the sum of $50.[438] The deed mentioned that this was more or less the same property that Frazier Storer had purchased from a James McDonald and his wife, Mary, on 2 April 1862. The quit claim deed was subsequently recorded in Muskingum County.

After Madison Howell moved to Missouri, he remained there for the rest of his life. Although he owned land in Dade County, he lived for a while in Springfield, Missouri, at 413 W. Clay Street. At the time of his death on March 19, 1909, he was living with his son, W.E. Howell, east of South Greenfield, Missouri.[439] He was buried in the Daughtry Cemetery in Dade County. The grave is not marked. The exact location of the grave within the cemetery is not known as of this writing.

Madison Howell's wife may have died before he did. She is not mentioned in his brief obituary. She may also be buried in Daughtry Cemetery, but we have no proof of this.

Madison and Elizabeth Howell had six children, five of whom lived to adulthood. In the 1900 Census, information was given that Elizabeth had had six children, five of which were still living. The children's names are taken from federal census records in Ohio (1860)[440] and Missouri (1870, 1880).[441] Their dates of birth are also mainly taken from census records.

---

[438] Muskingum County, OH, Deed Bk 54:306.

[439] Dade County Advocate (Greenfield, Dade Co., MO), 25 March 1909, p. 2, Missouri Historical Society, Jefferson City.

[440] 1860 federal census, free schedule, Muskingum County, OH, p. 111, family #793, dwelling #793.

[441] 1880 federal census, population schedule, Greene County, MO, p. 272, dwelling #190, family #157.

Madison Howell family about 1872. L-R: Martha, Madison, Willis, Mary, Chalmers, Elizabeth, and Lines.

+132   i.   Chalmers[5] Howard Howell, born 6 March 1854, in New Concord,Ohio.

133   ii.   Willis Elmo Howell, born November 1857, in Muskingum County, Ohio. He died in 1947, after spending most of his life farming in Dade County, Missouri. He is buried in Pennsboro Cemetery.[442] He married Mary Margaret Jordan 27 October 1878 in Dade County, Missouri.[443] She was born in 1860 and died in 1944 and is buried beside her husband.[444] Their known

---

[442] Headstone Inscription for Willis E. Howell, Pennsboro Cemetery, Section D, Dade County, MO.

[443] Dade County, MO, Marriage Record, copy in possession of author, Wallace.

[444] Headstone Inscription for Mary M. Howell, Pennsboro Cemetery, Section D, Dade County, MO.

children were W. C. (1880), John (1882), and Bertha May (1893).[445]

134   iii.   Martha J. Howell was born 1860 in Muskingum County, Ohio. She married Grundy L. Gibbons 23rd July 1875 in Dade County, Missouri.[446] They were married by a Rev. C. G. Gibbons, possibly a relative of the groom. Efforts to locate this couple in the 1880 Soundex for Missouri and immediate states to the south and west were not successful.

135   iv.   Lines W. Howell, born April 1863, in Muskingum County, Ohio. He married Clara V. Williams 4 January 1890, in Dade County, Missouri.[447] Their known children as of 1900 and 1910 were Harry D. (an adopted son born 1890), Roxie (1892), Millie E. (1894), Orville L. (1899) and Artie (c. 1903).[448]

136   v.   Mary Howell, born about 1865, in Muskingum County, Ohio. She was 5 years old when the census enumerator came to her parents' home on 23 June 1870.[449] She is not listed with the family in the 1880 census. She probably died after the 1870 census and before the 1880 census.

---

[445] 1900 federal census, population schedule, Dade County, MO, family #158, dwelling #158, ED 71, sheet 7.

[446] Dade County, MO, Marriage Record, copy in possession of author Wallace.

[447] Ibid.

[448] 1900 federal census, population schedule, Crawford County, KS (City of Pittsburg), vol. 13, ED 83, Sheet 18, 24; 1910 federal census soundex.

[449] 1870 federal census, population schedule, Dade County, MO, Marion Township, p. 36, family #21, dwelling #21.

137   vi.   Flora M. Howell, born January 1873, in Dade
County, Missouri. She married William B. Singer
in Dade County, Missouri at the home of her
parents.   The marriage date was 22 March
1891.[450]   The marriage record shows that
William's father was W.B. Singer. Their known
children as of 1900, 1910 and 1920 were Viola M.
(1892), Herschal (1895), Apha C. (1899), Eloie
(Elva), a son born about 1906 and Lora and Voda
(twins born about 1913).[451]

63. Benjamin[4] Howell (John[3], Benjamin[2], Hugh[1]) was born 8 March
1812 in Flushing Township, Belmont County, Ohio.[452] He died 18
February 1888,[453] and is buried at Windy Point Cemetery, Flushing
Township.[454] He married, (1), Elizabeth Willis,[455] who was born
1814/1815 in Ohio[456] and died 1862, and is buried in Flushing.[457]
He married (2) in Guernsey County[458] 24 October 1867, Sarah

---

[450] Dade County, MO, Marriage Record, copy in possession of author Wallace.

[451] 1900 federal census, population schedule, Dade County, MO, family #232,
dwelling #235, ED 67, sheet 12; 1910 federal census soundex; 1920 federal census
soundex.

[452] Johnson, The Howell Family History, p. 3.

[453] Ibid.

[454] Powell, Tombstone Inscriptions, p. 13.

[455] Johnson, The Howell Family History, p. 3.

[456] 1850 federal census, population schedule, Union Township, Belmont County,
OH, p. 462, dwelling #1397, family #1426.

[457] Johnson, The Howell Family History, p. 3.

[458] International Genealogical Index (IGI), LDS Ohio.

McElroy,[459] born 1829/1830 in Ohio.[460] Parents of the wives of Benjamin are unknown.

Benjamin is mentioned in the history of the local area in the following way:[461]

> John C. Howell, eldest son of Benjamin, who was the son of John Howell ...

The 1840 census of Union Township shows a Benjamin Howell of age 20-30 living with a female 20-30.[462] This family is quite likely our Benjamin and Elizabeth Howell. The 1850 census shows Benjamin with his wife, Elizabeth, and four children: Cyrus, Malinda, Elizabeth and Harvey.[463] The last census on which Benjamin appears is the 1870 census where he is shown with his second wife, Sarah, and children, Benjamin, Elizabeth, and Clara.[464]

Known children, natives of Ohio, of Benjamin and Elizabeth were:[465]

---

[459] Johnson, The Howell Family History, p. 3.

[460] 1870 federal census, population schedule, Union Township, Belmont County, OH, p. 366, dwelling #110, family #115. 1880 federal census, population schedule, Union Township, Belmont County, OH, p. 403c, dwelling #102, family #104.

[461] Caldwell, History of Belmont and Jefferson Counties, p. 380.

[462] 1840 federal census, population schedule, Union Township, Belmont County, OH, p. 157B.

[463] 1850 federal census, population schedule, Union Township, Belmont County, OH, p. 462, dwelling #1397, family #1426.

[464] 1870 federal census, population schedule, Union Township, Belmont County, OH, p. 366, dwelling #110, family #115.

[465] From the 1850 and 1870 census records cited above. And also 1860 federal census, population schedule, Union Township, Belmont County, OH, p. 71, dwelling #963, family #971.

138	i.	Ruth[5] E. Howell.
139	ii.	John Cyrus Howell, born 17 June 1841 in Union Township, Belmont County.[466]
140	iii.	Melinda Jane Howell, born 1843.
141	iv.	Elizabeth A. Howell, born 1845/46.
142	v.	Harvey W. Howell, born 1847/1848.
143	vi.	Clara Catherine Howell, born 7 July 1850.[467]
144	vii.	Benjamin Franklin Howell, born 1855/1856.

---

[466] Caldwell, <u>History of Belmont and Jefferson Counties</u>, p. 380.

[467] Johnson, <u>The Howell Family History</u>, p. 4.

CHAPTER SIX

AND POINTS WEST
GENERATIONS FIVE AND SIX

These are the grandchildren and great grandchildren of Abner Howell. They ventured to the west living in Illinois, Iowa, Missouri, Kansas, Oklahoma and Colorado. We have among them at least one, James, son of George, who fought in the Civil War.

77.   George[5] Howell (Alfred[4], Abner[3], William[2], Hugh[1]) was born 1837/1839[468] near Spratt, Rich Hill Township, Muskingum County, Ohio.[469]   He died in Iowa about August 1876.[470]   On 9 May 1864[471] he married his first cousin, Jane Lyons. She was born 23 February 1847; died 19 November 1933 in Lamont, Grant County,

---

[468] 1850 federal census, population schedule, Muskingum County, OH, p. 967, dwelling #194, family #194.

[469] 1850 census shows Ohio as place of birth. Since his father, Alfred, had been found living in Rich Hill Township in earlier census enumerations, it is assumed this is where George was born.

[470] Valley News (Lamont, Grant Co., OK), 23 November 1933, p. 1. Obituary of Jane (Lyons) (Howell) Young. The approximate date of death was calculated from information given in obituary.

[471] No official record of the marriage has been found. The year of the marriage is mentioned in Jane's obituary. The month, day, and year are verified on a page in the family bible (copyright date 1896) of John Jordan Young and Jane Young. Copy in possession of author Cameron.

Oklahoma.[472] After George's death, she married (2) John Jordan Young, born 26 March 1829 in England. He died 31 January 1924 in Lamont, Grant County, Oklahoma.[473]

Soon after their marriage, George and Jane moved to Kewanee, Illinois. Here they were converted and united with the Methodist Episcopal Church. They lived there for eight years, and their first three children were born there. By April 1871, when Nellie Ann was born, they had moved to Iowa where their last three children were born. According to Jane's obituary, Fred P. was 18 months old (born February 1875) when his father died. This information gives us an August 1876 date of death for George.

After George died, his widow took their six small children back home to Ohio where they were cared for either in foster homes or orphanages. Jane was appointed guardian of her children 12 August 1880.[474] On 30 October 1884,[475] she married John Jordan Young, son of Thomas and Martha (Jordan) Young. A traditional comment of family members is that in this second marriage Jane not only obtained for herself a husband and a father for her orphaned children, but the marriage also provided spouses for two of those children, i.e., Alva Austin Howell and Rosetta Howell, as indicated below.

The birth dates of the children of George and Jane Howell listed below are shown in the family bible of John Jordan and Jane (Lyons)

[472] Valley News (Lamont, Grant Co., OK), 23 November 1933, p. 1; obituary of Jane (Lyons) (Howell) Young.

[473] Death Certificate, Oklahoma State Board of Health Bureau of Vital Statistics, Registration District 27253, Register No. 27-29.

[474] Guernsey County, OH, Guardianship Documents, 1880, #3-211, Case 4652, 12 August 1880.

[475] Family bible of John Jordan and Jane (Lyons) (Howell) Young, copyright 1896, original in the possession of J. Wayne Young, Rt 1 Box 244, Barnsdall, OK 74002, and a transcript in the hands of author Cameron.

(Howell) Young,[476] and the guardianship papers.[477]   The places of birth are deduced from their mother's obituary.[478]

145   i.   Alva Austin[6] Howell, born 9 May 1865 in Kewanee, Henry County, Illinois and died 17 February 1930.[479]   He married his step-sister, Flora Young, daughter of John Jordan Young, and Ann (Perry) Young.

146   ii.   Martha Jane Howell, born 5 March 1867 in Kewanee, Henry County, Illinois and died 18 August 1918 in Rich Hill Township, Muskingum County, Ohio.[480]   She married 25 January 1887 in Salt Creek Township, John Stevenson McCutcheon.[481]

147   iii.   Rosetta Howell, born 31 March 1867 in Kewanee, Henry County, Illinois,[482] and died 28 January 1944 in Lamont, Grant County, Oklahoma.[483]

---

[476] Ibid.

[477]Guernsey County, OH, Guardianship documents.   Note that where those documents show dates of 29 February in years which were not leap years the authors arbitrarily changed the date to 28 February.

[478] Valley News (Lamont, Grant Co., OK), 23 November 1933, p. 1; obituary of Jane (Lyons) (Howell) Young.

[479] Family bible of John Jordan and Jane (Lyons) (Howell) Young.

[480] Death Certificate #50417, State of Ohio, Bureau of Vital Statistics, Ohio Historical Society, Columbus, OH.

[481] Family group record prepared March 1982 by Kathryn McCutcheon, 2750 So. River Road, Zanesville, OH 43701.

[482] Obituary.   Transcript in hands of author Cameron.

[483] Ibid.

She married 23 July 1885 in Evansville, Vanderburgh County, Indiana her step-brother, Joseph Willis Young.[484] Rosetta is the grandmother of author Robert Willis Cameron, who was given his grandfather's middle name as his middle name.

148   iv.   Nellie Anne Howell, born April 1871 in Iowa and died after November 1933.[485] She married a man by the name of Hahn.[486]

149   v.   James Andrew Howell, born 28 February 1873 in Iowa and died after November 1933 in Kaw City, Osage, County, Oklahoma.[487]

150   vi.   Fred P. Howell born 28 February 1875 in Iowa and he died after November 1933.[488]

The children of John Jordan and Jane (Lyons) (Howell) Young included:

151   i.   Howard Young, born 25 December 1885[489] in McCutchanville, Vanderburgh County,

---

[484] Vanderburgh County, IN, Marriage Book 13, p. 95.

[485] Valley News, obituary of Jane (Lyons) (Howell) Young.

[486] Ibid.

[487] Ibid.

[488] Ibid.

[489] Family bible of John Jordan and Jane (Lyons) (Howell) Young, corroborated by obituary in The Valley News.

Indiana;[490] died 19 April 1908[491] in St. Joseph, Missouri.[492]

152   ii.   Jesse E. Young, born 28 June 1887[493] in Center Township, Vanderburgh County, Indiana;[494] died 19 December 1977 in Caldwell, Canyon County, Idaho.[495]

105.   James[5] A. Howell (George[4], Abner[3], William[2], Hugh[1]) was probably born 25 September 1844 in Zanesville, Muskingum County, Ohio.[496] He died 5 April 1922 at the Soldier's and Sailor's Home in Monte Vista, Rio Grande County, Colorado, and is buried there at Homelake Cemetery.[497] He married Mary Lanning on 3 December

---

[490] The Valley News, Lamont, OK, obituary.

[491] Family bible of John Jordan and Jane (Lyons) (Howell) Young, and corroborated by obituary.

[492] Interview with daughter, Lora (Young) Tebow in Medford, OK, 24 September 1993. She stated that he died of a cancer on the back in a hospital in St. Joseph, MO, although his residence was in Lamont, OK.

[493] Family bible of John Jordan and Jane (Lyons) (Howell) Young; and corroborated by his obituary.

[494] The Idaho Free Press and The News Tribune (Caldwell, Canyon Co., ID), 19 December 1977, obituary. Even though the obituary states he was born in Zanesville, Ohio, all other evidence, including the 1900 and 1920 census records show him born in Indiana.

[495] The Idaho Free Press and The News Tribune, obituary.

[496] 1900 federal census, population schedule, Monte Vista, Rio Grande County, CO, ED #149, sheet #10, residence #129. Pension papers give birth year as 1842.

[497] Now Colorado State Veteran's Center, Homelake Cemetery certificate in file of James A. Howell, #642.

1865 in Andrew County, Missouri.[498]   She was born about 1851,[499] the daughter of Joseph and Indiana (Meek) Lanning[500] and died between 1 June 1892 (birth of last child) and 21 November 1896 (date James made application to Soldiers' and Sailors' Home).[501]

James, age 5, was first found in the 1850 census, living with his parents in Swan Township, Vinton County, Ohio.[502]   He also appeared in 1860, still living with the family in the same location, now aged 17.[503]   There is some variance between his birth year as carried in his pension file (1842) and that reported by the family (1844) and the census records. However, with a fixed marriage date of his parents as 9 January 1840 and two older sisters, the 1844 date is a more realistic figure. He may have "altered" his age a couple years when he went off to join the Infantry on 11 August 1862, signing up for 3 years.[504]

He was mustered into Company B, 90th Regiment of the Ohio Volunteers shortly after that, on 31 October 1862. He was listed as being in a convalescent hospital at Camp Nashville, Tennessee for the

[498] "Civil War Record," I.C. Number 1066225, Department of the Interior, Bureau of Pensions, National Archives and Records Service, Washington, D.C., file dated 11 October 1921; hereafter referred to as Pension Papers. Also Andrew County, MO, Marriage Record #2056, Book A:357.

[499] Age given as 19 in 1870 federal census, population schedule, Platte Township, Andrew County, MO, dwelling #434, family #436, p. 62.

[500] Saguache County Court, CO, Letters of Guardianship, #1861, Book 2:599, names James A. Howell as guardian for Arthur and Curtis Howell, minor heirs of Joseph Lanning, deceased.

[501] Colorado State Veteran's Center, James A. Howell file.

[502] 1850 federal census, population schedule, Swan Township, Vinton County, OH, dwelling #152, family #153, p. 654.

[503] 1860 federal census, population schedule, Swan Township, Vinton County, OH, dwelling #441, family #333, p. 294.

[504] Pension papers.

months of November and December 1862 ... probably with typhoid pneumonia fever. He returned to active duty in January 1863. Less than a year later on 19 September 1863, he was wounded during the first day of the Battle of Chicamagua (Chickamauga), Georgia near the Tennessee border when a shell struck his right leg.[505] The Battle of Chickamauga was one of the bloodiest of the war, engaging 58,222 Union troops and 66,326 Confederate troops. Each sustained a 28% loss (killed, wounded or missing).[506] The severity of James' wound led to the statement found in his pension file that he was, "carried off the field for dead." He was temporarily treated at a field hospital, which was later captured by the enemy. They destroyed records making it difficult for him to prove his injury when he applied for a pension. He also spent time in hospitals at Murfreesboro and Chattanooga, but it is not clear why or when these hospitalizations took place. However, he served his three years and was mustered out at Camp Harker, Tennessee on 13 June 1865. He had "grown up" during the Civil War. Entering the War at barely 18, he was now not quite 21. He was a young man 5 feet 5 to 6 inches tall, with dark hair and complexion; his eyes were hazel.

After his discharge, he went to Andrew County, Missouri to join the rest of his family after the end of the war. It was there he was married on 3 December 1865 to Mary Lanning.[507] His pension papers of 11 October 1921 state she was a member of the Presbyterian Church, but there was no church record of the marriage; instead they were married by a Justice of the Peace.

James and Mary first settled in Platte Township, Andrew County, where they appear in the census of 1870. James, farmer, is shown as

---

[505] Pension application papers dated 21 March 1888, deposition dated 21 January 1914.

[506] Mark May Boatner, III, The Civil War Dictionary (New York: David McKay, 1959), p. 152.

[507] Andrew County, MO, Marriage Record #2056, Book A:357.

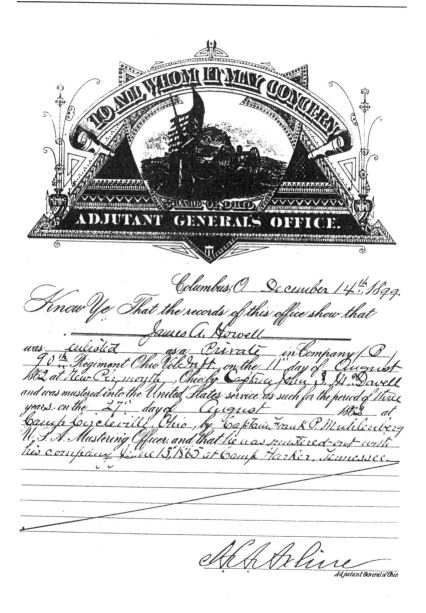

James A. Howell's discharge papers from the Civil War.

25 years old, with wife Mary, aged 19 and daughter, Ellen, age 2/12.[508]   Living next door were his parents,[509] while Mary's parents were not far away.[510] James' sister, Eliza Jane, now married to Burrows Powell, was living in the nearby community of Whitesville.[511] Sister Sarah and her husband, Edmond Cone Brooke, and their two young children were also nearby.[512]

By 1880 James and Mary were living in Lincoln Township, Linn County, Kansas, just across the border and about 140 miles south of their Missouri residence. In their household were 5 children: Ella W., 9; Lorren, 8; Rosa, 4; Joseph, 2; and Kimble J., 3/12.[513]   It is curious that neither census year shows a son, Arthur, reported by the family to be the eldest child.   James also states in his application papers to the Veteran's Home that he had a son, Arthur.   Whether Arthur was simply not listed or whether he was living elsewhere is unknown.   He does not show up in the households of either James' parents or other married siblings living in the Andrew County area. By 1880 that included his sister, Sarah, husband Edmond Brooke and family,[514] brother John W. and wife Lucinda,[515] and siblings Ambrose, Alfred, and Eliza J. living in one household with Ambrose

---

[508] 1870 federal census, population schedule, Platte Township, Andrew County, MO, dwelling #434, family #436, p. 62

[509] Ibid., dwelling #433, family #435, p. 62.

[510] Ibid., dwelling #129, family #131, p. 19.

[511] 1870 federal census, population schedule, Whitesville, Andrew County, MO, dwelling #88, family #90, p. 13.

[512] Ibid., dwelling #295, family #300, p. 43.

[513] 1880 federal census, population schedule, Lincoln Township, Linn County, KS, dwelling #11, family #11, ED 126, p. 2.

[514] 1880 federal census population schedule, Platte Township, Andrew County, MO, dwelling (not given), family #99, p. 11.

[515] Ibid., Subdistrict 44, dwelling #13, family #15, p. 2.

as head of family.[516] A fourth female, Hannah, is also listed in the household as a sister, but it seems more likely she was the daughter of Eliza whose husband Burrows Powell had disappeared from the scene sometime after the 1870 census.

By 1888, James and family had moved to Colorado. Their last child, Curtis, was born 1 June 1892 in Lamar, Prowers County, Colorado. James was widowed by 21 November 1896 when he made application to the Soldiers' and Sailors' Home at Monte Vista in Rio Grande County.[517] It took until 4 December 1899 for him to be admitted to that facility. At this point he would still have had several minor children. It is not known how they were provided for. However, on 25 July 1898, Letters of Guardianship were issued to James in Saguache County, naming Arthur and Curtis Howell (the oldest and the youngest children), as minor heirs of Joseph Lanning, deceased.[518] The extent of this inheritance from their grandfather Lanning is not known.

For the next 23 years he was a resident of the Home, but papers in his file indicate he did take periodic furloughs. On at least two occasions, 1903 and 1904, he was visiting in Newport, Andrew County, Missouri. We know from the obituaries of his brothers, Alfred and Ambrose, that they lived in Andrew County until their respective deaths in 1936 and 1937.[519]

It is not clear when he first started receiving a pension for his service in the Civil War. In a deposition in his pension file, he stated he first made application in 1865. However, the first application found in his pension file was dated 21 March 1888. The first reference to "my pay," was found in his file at the Soldiers' and Sailors' Home dated

---

[516] Ibid., Empire Township, dwelling #58, family #60, p. 8.

[517] Colorado State Veteran's Center, file #642.

[518] Saguache County Court, CO, Letters of Guardianship, #1861, Book 2:599.

[519] <u>Savannah Reporter</u> (Savannah, Andrew Co., MO), 28 February 1936, p. 5, and 4 June 1937, p. 5.

20 May 1901, when he referred to his pay for March, $25.[520]
However, additional application forms were found after that date as
additional provisions were made through new legislation. Apparently,
increases were allowed in 1907, 1912 and 1920. The last entry in his
pension file was a letter from his son, James K. Howell of Hooper,
Alamosa County, Colorado to the Commissioner of Pensions in
Washington, D.C. requesting unpaid funds due James after his death
to pay for small outstanding debts. He cited approval granted under
the Act of 1 May 1920 to increase his father's pension to $72 per
month.

Known and likely children of James A. and Mary (Lanning) Howell
include:

153   i.   Arthur S.[6] Howell, born February 1867,[521]
                     probably in Andrew County, Missouri. He married
                     (1) Mary L. whom he divorced 2 January
                     1903.[522] He married (2) Nora Sisemore on 1
                     May 1903 in Rio Grande County.[523] Between
                     marriages, he was found living as a lodger in a
                     hotel in Colorado Springs in the 1900 census.[524]
                     He apparently inherited something from his
                     grandfather, Joseph Lanning, since he was named
                     along with his youngest brother, Curtis in Letters
                     of Guardianship issued to his father in Saguache

---

[520] Colorado State Veteran's Center, file #642.

[521] 1900 Colorado census soundex, Precinct 36, El Paso County, Colorado
Springs, ED 29, p. 9, line 73.

[522] Denver, CO, District Court, Division 1.

[523] Rio Grande County, CO, marriage license #27248.

[524] 1900 Colorado Census Soundex, Precinct 36, Colorado Springs, El Paso
County, ED 29, p. 9, line 73. Listed as born 1867 in Ohio (in error?).

County, Colorado on 25 July 1898 regarding the trust of his estate.[525]

154   ii.   Ellen (Ella W.) Howell, born May 1870, Platte Township, Andrew County.[526] She died before 11 October 1921 when her father listed his children in his pension application of that date.

155   iii.   Sherman Howell, born February 1872, probably in Andrew County.[527] He died before 11 October 1921 when his father listed his children in his pension application of that date.

156   iv.   Loren Howell, born about 1872.[528] He died 15 April 1936 in Reno, Nevada.[529]

157   v.   Rose Anna (Dolly?)[530] Howell, born 19 March 1876.[531]

158   vi.   Joseph Howell, born about 1878.[532]

---

[525] Saguache County Court, CO, Letters of Guardianship, #1861, Book 2:599.

[526] 1870 federal census, population schedule, Platte Township, Andrew County, MO, dwelling #434, family #436, p. 62.

[527] 1900 Colorado Census Soundex, Las Animas County, ED 67, p. 8, line 95, listed a Sherman Hully, b. 1872 in Kansas. This seems to be a likely match.

[528] 1880 federal census, population schedule, Lincoln Township, Linn County, KS, dwelling #11, family #11, ED 126, p. 2.

[529] Information provided by family.

[530] "Dolly" was listed among James' children in his statement of 11 October 1921, while no mention of Rose was made.

[531] Information provided by family.

[532] 1880 federal census, Lincoln Township, Linn County, KS.

159   vii.   Kimble J. Howell, born March 1880;[533] probably
                      died   before 22 January 1882.[534]

160   viii.   James Kimball Howell, born 22 January 1882. He
                      married Mollie Amick on 13 February 1903 in
                      Salida, Saguache County, Colorado. He died 13
                      February 1960 in Long Beach, California.[535]

161   ix.   Curtis Everett Howell, born 1 June 1892 in Lamar,
                      Prowers County, Colorado. In 1898, he along with
                      his brother, Arthur, inherited something from his
                      grandfather, Joseph Lanning, since he was named
                      in Letters of Guardianship issued to his father in
                      Saguache County.[536] He married Martha Jane
                      Amick on 25 November 1908 in Garnett, Rio
                      Grande County. He was a lumberman at the time
                      of his marriage. In 1910, they moved to Idaho
                      where they remained until 1919 when they moved
                      to Santa Cruz, California. He died 23 September
                      1969 in Watsonville, Santa Cruz County,
                      California.[537]

132. Chalmers Howard[5] Howell (Madison[4], Abner[3], William[2], Hugh[1])
the oldest child of Madison Howell was born 6 March 1854 in New

---

[533] Ibid.

[534] No other mention of this child was found. He was not listed in father's
pension papers either as a living or deceased child. Also a son with similar name,
James Kimball was born 22 January 1882.

[535] Information provided by family.

[536] Saguache County Court, CO, Letters of Guardianship, #1861, Book 2:599.

[537] Information provided by family.

Concord, Ohio.[538]   He died 23 October 1921 in Colorado Springs, Colorado where he was also buried. He was married first to Marinda M. Worthen, daughter of Ephraim Worthen and Sarah German, 9 September 1876, in Barton County, Missouri. Marinda was born 16 January 1856, in Meigs County, Ohio. She died 26 February 1898, near Cedar Vale, Kansas. Burial took place in Cowley County, Kansas. Chalmers married for the second time to O. Emma DeShazo Sleeth (1866-1944) about 1900. She is buried beside her husband in Colorado Springs.

Chalmers spent the early years of his life in Muskingum County where he attended school and helped out on his parent's small farm. About 1867, Chalmers moved with his parents to Dade County, Missouri. When the census was taken in 1870, he was listed as a 16-year old farm laborer, who was living in the household of Madison Howell.[539] The census taker also recorded that he attended school.

Chalmers, who was also known as Charles or Charley, met a girl from neighboring Barton County, Missouri. He married her 9 September 1876, in Barton County.[540]   Her name was Marinda Minnie Worthen. She had been born in Meigs County, Ohio 16 January 1856, the daughter of Ephraim and Sarah (German) Worthen.[541]   The Worthen family dates back to Colonial New Hampshire and Massachusetts. The presence of Marinda's ancestor, George Worthen in Massachusetts, has been documented as early as 1640.[542]

---

[538] Death Certificate for Chalmers H. Howell.

[539] 1870 federal census, population schedule, Marion Township, Dade County, MO, p. 36, dwelling #21, family #21.

[540] Barton County, MO, Marriage Record, copy in possession of author Richard Wallace.

[541] 1870 federal census, population schedule, Golden Grove Township, Barton Co., MO, p. 6, dwelling #33, family #33; Meigs Co., OH Marriage Records 1-177.

[542] Richard W. Musgrove, History of the Town of Bristol, Grafton County, New Hampshire, vol. II (Bristol, NH: author, 1904), p. 466.

Marinda's father was originally from Enfield, Grafton County, New Hampshire.

When the census was taken in 1880, Chalmers Howell was farming in Dade County - Marion Township.[543] By that time, he and his wife had two small sons - William C. (age 2) and John H. (age 3 months).

After 1880 but before 1885, the Chalmers Howell family made the decision to move farther west. This time they moved to Cowley County, Kansas - Otter Township, just over the Chatauqua County line. The town of Cedar Vale is very close to that line, and this is where the author's grandmother always said she was from, even though she was born in Cowley County. Cedar Vale was the closest town of any size to the family farm.

In those days, the State of Kansas took what was called an agricultural census midway between the federal census years. In 1885, this census revealed that Chalmers was still farming and his family had increased by two girls.[544] These were Alpha May (age 3), who would go by her middle name, and "Olie" (age 2 months). "Olie's" full name was Mary Viola, but to family and friends she was known as Ola.

In 1891, a photograph was taken of Chalmers' family. The photo includes all family members, except the youngest child (Ward D.) who had not yet been born. In the front are Chalmers, holding Myrtle, Marinda, Ola, and Mabel. Standing in back are May, William ("Will"), and John.

The 1895 Census gives a complete picture of the C.H. Howell family.[545] Since 1885, three more children had been born. These

---

[543] 1880 federal census, population schedule, Marion Township, Dade County, MO, ED 13, p. 6, dwelling #48, family #51.

[544] 1885 Kansas Census, Cowley County, Otter Township, State Historical Society, Topeka.

[545] 1895 Kansas Census, Cowley County, Otter Township, State Historical Society, Topeka.

Chalmers Howell family - 1891. L-R: Myrtle, Chalmers, May, Marinda, Will, Ola, John, and Mabel.

were Mabel (age 9), Myrtle (age 4) and Ward D. (age 4 months).

Tragedy struck the Howell family not very long after the 1895 Census. In the short space of a year ending February 1898, three members of the family met untimely deaths. The first to go was Ward who was only two years old when he died early in 1897. On 5 April, her birthday, May died after a "lengthy illness."[546] Perhaps the most tragic was the death of Marinda Howell on 26 February 1898.[547] She was only 42 years old. She was buried in Cedar Creek Cemetery, Cowley County, Kansas.

After these unfortunate events, we next find the Howell family living in Cedar Vale on Doane Street.[548] The time was 2 June 1900.

---

[546] <u>Cedar Vale Commercial</u> (Cedar Vale, Chatauqua Co., KS), 9 April 1897, p. 1, State Historical Society, Topeka.

[547] <u>Cedar Vale Commercial</u> (Cedar Vale, Chatauqua Co., KS), 4 March 1898, p. 1, State Historical Society, Topeka.

[548] 1900 federal census, population schedule, Chatauqua County, KS, ED 3, sheets 2 & 3, dwelling #37, family #37.

L-R: Myrtle, Ola, and Mabel Howell - about 1904.

Chalmers was a widower, whose occupation was "day laborer." The only children still at home were daughters Ola, Mabel, and Myrtle.

Probably not long after the census was taken, Chalmers married for the second time. This time he married a widow, O. Emma (De Shazo) Sleeth.[549] This marriage would produce two children, the first born in 1902.

Before he died in 1921, Chalmers and his second family moved to Colorado Springs, Colorado. This move probably took place after 1910. He was living at 1302 E. Platte Avenue when he died on 23 October.[550] He was buried in Evergreen Cemetery of that city.[551] His wife, Emma, survived her husband by about 23 years. She died

---

[549] Harriet Campbell, 801 Faulkner St., Wichita, KS 67203, to author, 7 March 1978.

[550] Death Certificate for Chalmers Howell.

[551] Headstone Inscription for Chalmers H. Howell, Evergreen Cemetery, Colorado Springs, CO.

in 1944 and is buried next to her husband.[552] Her stone reflects an 1866 date of birth.

Chalmers and Marinda Howell had seven children as follows:

162   i.   William Chalmers[6] Howell, born 8 August 1877, Dade County, Missouri; married 1906, Pueblo, Colorado, Retta ----;[553] died, 27 February 1978, Portland, Oregon, entombment in that city's Lincoln Memorial Mausoleum;[554] children: Glen, William, Jr.

163   ii.   John H. Howell, born February 1880, Dade County, Missouri; never married; died 1942, Wichita, Kansas, burial in Wichita Park Cemetery.[555] He worked in gold and silver mines in Colorado, and prospected for gold on his own in the mountains near his cabin at Breckinridge.

164   iii.   Alpha May Howell, born 5 April 1882, Dade County, Missouri; died 5 April 1897, Cowley County, Kansas, burial in Cedar Creek Cemetery, Cowley County.[556]

---

[552] Headstone Inscription for O. Emma Howell, Evergreen Cemetery, Colorado Springs, CO.

[553] Fiftieth Wedding Invitation (Mr. & Mrs. William C. Howell), copy in possession of author Wallace.

[554] Death Certificate for William C. Howell, 27 February 1958, State File No. 2136, Oregon State Health Division, Portland, OR 97207.

[555] Headstone Inscription for John Howell, Wichita Park Cemetery, Wichita, KS.

[556] Cedar Vale Commercial, 9 April 1897.

165   iv.   Mary Viola Howell, born 13 February 1885,
                    Cowley County, Kansas; never married; died 6
                    August 1908, of a brain tumor, in Wichita, Kansas,
                    burial in Cedar Creek Cemetery, Cowley
                    County.[557]

+166   v.   Mabel Ann Howell, born 20 February 1887,
                    Cowley County, Kansas.

+167   vi.   Myrtle Coretta Howell, born 3 August 1890,
                    Cowley County, Kansas.

168   vii.   Ward D. Howell, born 18 December 1894, Cowley
                    County, Kansas; died, 12 February 1897, Cowley
                    County, Kansas, burial in Cedar Creek Cemetery,
                    Cowley County.[558]

Chalmers and Emma Howell had two children.

169   i.   Stanley Howell, born 26 April 1902, Chatauqua
                    County, Kansas; married Lois ---; children: Donald
                    Howard, Patricia, Betty Jo, and Robert.[559]

170   ii.   Grace Howell, born 1 January 1904, Chatauqua
                    County, Kansas; married (1) 2 July 1925, Roy
                    Keffer, (2) 4 April 1948, Ted Moore; died 28
                    February 1978, Canon City, Colorado; children:
                    Barbara Janet (1926), Clyde Warren (1928).[560]

---

[557] Cedar Vale Commercial (Cedar Vale, Chatauqua Co., KS), 14 August 1908,
p. 1, State Historical Society, Topeka.

[558] Cedar Vale Commercial.

[559] Harriet Campbell, 7 March 1978.

[560] Ibid.

Ward and Myrtle Howell - 1895.

166. Mabel Ann[6] Howell (Chalmers[5], Madison[4], Abner[3], William[2], Hugh[1]) was born 20 February 1887[561] in Cowley County, Kansas - Otter Township. She died 21 November 1973, in Wichita, Kansas. Her husband, William Cecil Jones, was born 12 June 1886, in Sedan, Kansas, the son of O. Jones and Orra Ann Adams. Mabel and Cecil married 15 October 1905, at Sedan, Kansas. Cecil Jones died April 1941, in Wichita, Kansas. Both are buried in Wichita Park Cemetery.

Mabel spent her early girlhood on the family farm. After her mother died in 1898, she moved with her father and two sisters (Ola and Myrtle) to Cedar Vale, where she attended grade school. At the age of 14, she left home and went to Sedan, Kansas where she learned to sew from a dressmaker. She tried to finish high school, but found it impossible to attend school and earn a living at the same time. Although she always regretted the decision to drop school, she did become an expert seamstress and tailor. It was in Sedan that she met her future husband.

On 15 October 1905, she married William Cecil Jones at Sedan, Kansas.[562] Cecil, as he was called, was born 12 June 1886 in Sedan, the son of Orange Vandever Lemon Jones and Orra Ann Adams.[563] He learned his trade as a printer while working for a brother-in-law in Cedar Vale. With his new wife, he moved to Wichita to work, but returned to Cedar Vale in 1912 when he bought the County Liner and published it successfully.

In 1924 the family moved to Wichita where Cecil was foreman on The Wichita Eagle. He helped nephew Harold W. Wallace and son-in-law Scott K. Campbell gain apprenticeships in the printing trade at the Eagle. They continued with this line of work throughout their working lives.

---

[561] 1900 federal census, population schedule, Chautauqua Co., KS, e.d. 3, sheets 2 & 3, family #37, dwelling #37.

[562] Chautauqua County Marriage Record, copy in possession of author Wallace.

[563] Harriet Campbell, 101 S. Union Blvd., Colorado Springs, CO 80910, to Richard Wallace, 24 September 1992.

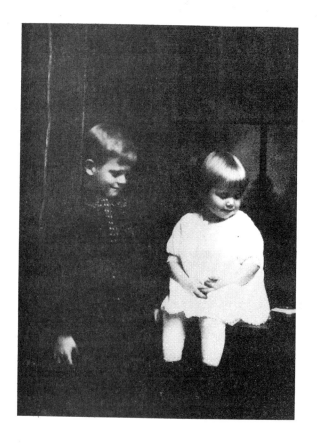

Harold and Mabel Wallace - about 1917

In Wichita the Jones family owned a house at 1142 Amidon which is directly across the street from Sim Memorial Golf Course. Here son Billy Jones learned the skills that led to many amateur golfing championships, including the Kansas State Amateur Championship title about 1940. He was also state high school champion the three years he attended North High School. He and his father also won father and son tournaments.

Cecil Jones suffered a heart attack in April 1941. He died the same day. He was 54 years old. He was buried in Wichita Park Cemetery.[564]

After her husband's death, Mabel (Aunt Mabel to the author's family) moved to a house at 1408 W. Murdock in Wichita. This home was close to a bend of the Arkansas River in the west Riverside area of Wichita in a park-like setting of big trees and wide boulevards.

Mabel Jones survived her husband by 32 years. She continued to live at the house on Murdock Street where she had developed and rented out several apartments. She died 21 November 1973,[565] of the debilitating effects of old age. She was buried next to her husband.

Mabel and Cecil Jones had two children:[566]

171   i.   Harriet Madeline[7] Jones, born 8 November 1916, in Wichita, Kansas; married Scott K. Campbell 9 August 1932, in Wichita, Kansas; children: James Michael Campbell (1937); Madelyn Cecil Campbell (1943).

---

[564] Tombstone inscription for W. Cecil Jones, Wichita Park Cemetery, Wichita, KS.

[565] Tombstone Inscription for Mabel A. Jones, Wichita Park Cemetery, Wichita, KS.

[566] Harriet Campbell to author, 24 September 1992.

172   ii.   William Cecil Jones, Jr. born 19 May 1922; never married, joined the U.S. Navy in 1942; died in service in Italy 3 August 1944, of polio; burial in Wichita Park Cemetery after the end of World War II. He is buried by his parents.

167. Myrtle Coretta[6] Howell (Chalmers[5], Madison[4], Abner[3], William[2], Hugh[1]) was born 3 August 1890[567] on her father's farm in Cowley County, Kansas. She died 21 January 1971, in Wichita, Kansas, and is entombed in Wichita Park Mausoleum. She married Reece J. Wallace 24 May 1908, in Wichita, Kansas. He was born 2 January 1888, near Cedar Vale, Kansas, the son of John W. Wallace and Mary J. Waters. He died 2 March 1982, in Wichita, Kansas, and is entombed next to his wife.

Myrtle attended a one room school which the author and his grandmother visited about 1960. At that time, the building was being used to store grain. The building was still in pretty good shape, all things considered. The chalkboards were still in place, silently waiting for another teacher or student to diagram a sentence or solve a math problem.

The nostalgic visit to Cowley County also included a visit to the family home, long since sold, in Otter Township. The house, a fairly typical farm home of the late nineteenth century in shape and appearance, was abandoned. An interesting finding was the hardy variety of roses that was still growing in the yard over 60 years after they had been planted.

Myrtle continued her schooling after her father moved to Cedar Vale, Kansas, not far from the farm in Cowley County. She graduated from

---

[567] 1900 federal census, population schedule, Chautauqua County, KS, ED 3, sheets 2 & 3, dwelling #37, family #37.

the Cedar Vale Public Schools 19 April 1907.[568]   Her teacher was
V. Bertha Harris and the school principal was N.A. Baker.

Myrtle would be considered short by today's taller women. She was
5'2" tall. Her complexion was fair and she had red hair. As a
teenager and young adult, her long, red hair extended to the small of
her back when it was undone. The fashion of the day was for women
to wear their hair "up" - held in place by pins. The best way to
describe their appearance would be to use the term "Gibson girl."

While attending school in Cedar Vale, she met her future husband,
Reece John Wallace. He had been born near Cedar Vale, Kansas 2
January 1888, the son of John William and Mary Jane (Waters)
Wallace.[569]   The parents had been residents of the area since the
1870's. John Wallace was a farmer, who lived in Jefferson Township
(Chautauqua County). Although he had lived several places before he
came to Kansas, John's birthplace was Clay County, Missouri.[570] His
wife was born in Pennsylvania.[571]

Reece Wallace and Myrtle Howell married 24 May 1908[572] in
Wichita, Kansas. The marriage took place in the home of William
and Mabel (Howell) Jones, brother-in-law and sister of the bride.
They also served as witnesses to the ceremony.

---

[568] Certificate of Attainment issued to Myrtle Howell by the Cedar Vale, KS
Public Schools, original in possession of author Richard Wallace.

[569] 1900 federal census, population schedule, Jefferson Township, Chautauqua
County, KS, ED 7, sheet ---, dwelling #158, family #158.

[570] A.T. Andreas, History of the State of Kansas (Chicago, IL: author, 1883), p.
1225.

[571] 1880 federal census, population schedule, Harrison Township, Chautauqua
County, KS, p. 329, dwelling #109, family #109.

[572] Marriage Record issued by St. John's Episcopal Church, Wichita, KS,
original in possession of author Wallace.

The newlyweds' first home was in Granite, Oklahoma, where Reece had recently moved with his parents. Granite is located in Greer County, and is roughly 100 miles southwest of Oklahoma City. His father had a small three-room house built for the young couple.

In Granite, Reece tried his hand at cotton farming for a couple of seasons. After these crops were blown and dusted out, he elected to make a career change that would prove to be permanent. He took a U.S. Civil Service Commission examination 22 October 1909, and was notified 13 December 1909 that he had passed.[573] He was appointed a mail carrier 24 April 1910 in Wichita, Kansas by then Postmaster W.C. Edwards. In those days mail carriers earned an average of $1100.00 a year, and first class postage was two cents an ounce.[574] When he retired in 1956, Reece had logged over 46 years of service with the Postal Service, and had worked his way up to be chief superintendent of mail carriers in the Wichita office.

Working outside the home was not an option available to many married women when Myrtle married in 1908. Consequently, she spent her life making a comfortable home for her husband and family. She was an excellent cook, who could prepare a fine meal and make it look easy. This is not to say it was easy. It simply looked easy when she did it.

The author remembers with particular enjoyment the chicken and noodles his grandmother prepared. The noodles were made from scratch - mixed, hand-rolled, cut, and dried. Childhood illnesses were guaranteed to produce a batch of grandma's chicken and noodles, personally delivered in a giant mason jar. We weren't Jewish, but those folks weren't the only people with their own special brand of penicillin.

---

[573] U.S. Civil Service Commission to Reece Wallace 13 December 1909, original in possession of author Wallace.

[574] "U.S. Mail Rides on Changing Tide," The Wichita Eagle, 31 January 1972.

Grandmother also made a cole slaw concoction that I've never seen duplicated anywhere. No, I'm not talking about those creamy cole slaws that are found in abundance. Her slaw was made from finely chopped cabbage, vinegar, spices, bacon drippings and bacon bits. Um Good!

Before we dispose of grandmother's cooking, and I'm about ready for a snack myself, she was a superior baker of pies - all from scratch - including berry pies of all kinds and a fine mincemeat pie.

The Wallaces spent most of their married life in two Wichita homes. By far the largest amount of time was spent in a house at 1015 Hendryx on the near west side of Wichita, about a block east of Seneca. This house, which had been expanded several times over the years, got caught up in the Kellogg Street expansion in the 1950's. The land where the house used to be is now part of the Seneca Street interchange.

Reece and Myrtle moved to the second home in 1956. It was located at 1325 W. 27th Street South. Here they would remain for the rest of their lives. Myrtle died suddenly there in the early morning of 21 January 1971 of either a stroke or a heart attack.[575] She had suffered from heart trouble for 20 years. Several years before her death, she had begun to exhibit the symptoms of a patient who suffers from hardening of the arteries - forgetfulness, etc. She was entombed in Wichita Park Mausoleum.

Her husband remained in the home on 27th Street for another 11 years. He died of metastatic cancer of the prostate at St. Francis Hospital in Wichita 2 March 1982. He was entombed next to his wife.

Myrtle (Howell) and Reece Wallace had three children, as follows:

---

[575] Death Certificate for Myrtle (Howell) Wallace, 21 January 1971, Kansas State Department of Health, Topeka, KS, State file #71-1405.

173   i.   Reece John[7] Wallace, Jr. born and died the same day in January 1909 in Granite, Oklahoma.[576]

174   ii.   Harold Ward Wallace, born 16 December 1910 in Wichita, Kansas; married Sydrena E. Ulsh 21 March 1934 in Newton, Kansas; children: Harold Ward Wallace, Jr. (1937); Richard Edwin Wallace (1939).

175   iii.   Mabel Isbell Wallace, born 2 June 1915 in Wichita, Kansas; married (1) Eugene Hund 24 June 1936, (2) Carl Mauel 14 May 1939, (3) Paul E. Hopper 2 July 1949 in Liberty, Missouri; children: Carma L. Mauel (1944. She was later adopted by P. Hopper); Brian Paul Hopper (1952).

---

[576] Family Record kept by Mary J. Wallace, original in possession of author Wallace.

CHAPTER SEVEN

CONCLUSION

This branch of the Howell family has participated, either actively or passively, in nearly 300 years of the European experience in North America. We first found them in the Province of New Jersey, nearly two generations before the American Revolution. These early Howells were predominantly farmers, who mostly cultivated small acreages. Some of these early ancestors lacked a formal education and could not read or write, not unusual for that period. Farming continued to be the main occupation of family members well into the nineteenth century, as were the vast majority of other Americans.

In religious matters, we have found that the early Howells were either Quakers or Baptists, whose form of worship did not conform with the practices of the established Church of England. We can't be certain, but religious persecution may have been a factor that led to the immigration of Howells to America in the first place.

Change is always difficult for people, but the Howells recognized the need for change by coming to America in a time when safe passage across the Atlantic was likely, but by no means certain. Once in America, they continued to recognize that the need for change is a repetitive process. However, their later changes/moves were probably motivated more by either economic necessity or improvement than by religious problems with the established Church.

During the time of the French and Indian War, Hugh Howell and others of the same surname, moved from Hunterdon County, New Jersey to Loudoun County, Virginia. While in Virginia, the Revolutionary War broke out, and many Loudoun County residents supported the cause for independence. Included in this group were

Hugh's son, William, and William's son, Reuben. We have learned that many Loudoun County residents were inspired by the revolutionary preachings of the Rev. John Marks, a Baptist preacher, whose daughter married William Howell.

The treaty that ended the Revolutionary War in 1783 ceded the area known as the Northwest Territories to the infant United States. Part of this large land area became the State of Ohio in 1803. This new state would soon become a magnet for thousands of settlers, including some of Hugh Howell's children and grandchildren, who used the river system to travel to their new homes. Subsequent moves by later generations took the Howell name across the Mississippi into Missouri, Kansas, Oklahoma, Colorado, and over the Rockies to California.

Appendix A

Selected Documents

SELECTED DOCUMENTS

Many documents were found and examined while tracing this Howell family as far back in time as possible. Only a few are presented here in transcribed form. We have selected some of the earliest plus a liberal sprinkling of those involving Abner[3] (William,[2] Hugh[1]). Abner was an especial challenge since he died intestate. However, because he owned property, a probate file was left. His probate file, the laws of inheritance in Ohio during that period, and marriage records of his children served to enable us to reconstruct his family. It was only after this had been done that confirmation came in the form of a Bible record owned by Abner Howell, Jr., which served to verify our work and to provide exact birth dates for Abner's children. For readers who would like more details on this work, see Carmen J. Finley, "Howells of Muskingum County, Ohio: Correlating and Interpreting Evidence to Reconstruct a Family," National Genealogical Society Quarterly 81 (June 1993): 194-203.

As was common during this time period, many people were not able to read or write well enough to spell their own names. However, they did make "their mark," usually an "x," on the original document. In its transcribed form, just an "x" appears here to distinguish literate from non-literate signers.

Hugh Howell's Will[1]
6 March 1777
Loudoun County, Virginia

In the name of God Amen the Sixth day of March in the Year of our Lord one thousand Seven Hundred and Seventy Seven I Hugh Howell of Shelburn Parish in the County of Loudoun and State of Virginia farmer being Very sick and weak in body but of perfect mind and memory thanks be Given to God calling into mind the mortallity of my Body and knowing that it is appointed for all men once to die do make and ordain this my last will and testament, that is to say Principally and first of all I Give and recommend my Soul into the hands of almighty God that Gave it and my body I recommend to the Earth to be buried in a decent christian burial. Imprimis I will and desire that all my just Debts which I shall owe at the time of my Decease togather with my Burial Charges be duly observed and paid I do hereby Constitute Depute and appoint William Howell my son and Timothy Hixon both of the same place to be my Sole executors of this my Last will and testament to act jointly or Severally as the Case may Require. Item I give and bequeath unto Margaet Howell my well beloved wife all my Land together with all my moveable Estate as long as she remains my Widow or during her natural life and in Case She Should marry to have what the Law allows a third Item and after her Decease the Land with all the moveable Estate be sold and jointly divided among all his Children Andrew Howell abner Howell John Howell Benjamin Howell Daniel Howell Rubin Howell and Rachel & ann Howell each having an equal Share (all my Land and Estate to be) by her freely possessed and enjoyed and I do utterly disallow revoke and disannul all and Every other former testament & will Legacies and Bequest and Executor by me any ways before named willed and bequeathed, ratifing and Confirming This and no other, to be my last will and Testament, in witness whereof I have hereunto set my hand and Seal the Day and year above written.
Signed Sealed Published Pronounced and Declared by the said Hugh Howell as his Last will and testament In presence of

---

[1] Loudoun County, VA, Will Bk B:176.

Francis Haugue
William Hixon
Timothy Hixon

Hugh x Howell (seal)

At a Court held for Loudoun County May 12th 1777:

This Will of Hugh Howell Deceased was proved by the Affirmation of Francis Haugue and oath of Timothy Hixon witnesses thereto and ordered to be Recorded And on the motion of William Howell, and Timothy Hixon Executors ...[2]

---

[2] The earliest, but unproven notes we found stated:

> Hugh Howell, born 17 April 1659 Wales, emigrated 1699, died 14 September 1745 Sussex County, age 86 on tombstone, buried Baptistown (?). Sons Hugh Howell born 1720, died 1777, married Margaret Hixson; Sampson Howell born 17 December 1717 Sussex County.

From the Hunterdon Genealogical Services, P.O. Box 334, Ringoes, New Jersey 98551; Historical Society Howell folder.

Flavious J. Howell Bible Record[3]

1) Hannah Elizabeth Howell was borned on Friday the 15 day of August 1834

2) Thompson Jessie Howell was bornd on Thursday the 30 day of July 1835.

3) Amanda Ann Howell was bornd on Thursday 23 day of February 1837.

4) Rodney Craven Howell was bornd on Monday the 19 of November 1838.

5) George William Howell was borned on Tuesday 22 day of September 1840.

6) Mary Dorcus Howell was borned on Sunday the 18 day of September 1842.

7) Townshend Berkely Howell was borned on Tuesday the 8 day of October 1844.

8) Benton Dallas Howell was borned on Monday the 12 day of October 1846.

9) Eliza Rachel Howell was borned on the 30 day of July 1848.

10) Laura Rosanna Howell was borned on Tuesday the 21 day of December, 1852.

---

[3] Found by Phyllis M. Darr, P.O. Box 55, Round Hill, VA 22141. Mrs. Darr had been married to Howard Thompson, son of Martha Howell Thompson, granddaughter of Jesse Howell. Flavious Howell was the son of Joseph W. Howell, grandson of David Howell and great-grandson of Jesse and Hannah (James) Howell. The first group of children in this record, 1) through 10), are the children of Jesse and Hannah's son, Craven James Howell. The second group, following 10), are the children of Jesse and Hannah.

Rodney C. Howell died december 16th 1873 at Baxter Springs cherikee county Kansas aged 34 years 11 months & 27 days buried at Fort Scott

Levi Howell son of Jesse Howell & Hannah his wife was born on Friday the 10 day of July 1795 and Died the 14th of July.

Abel Howell was born on Friday 30th of September 1796 & Died 25th of October 1798.
Elizah Howell was born on Saturday 14th of December 1799.

Anna Howell was born on Wendsday (sic) the 6th of January 1802.

David Howell was born on Saturday the 17th of September 1803.

Craven Howell was born on Sunday the 13th of October 1805.

Eda Howell was born on Wendsday (sic) the 16th of December 1807.

Emily Howell was born on Sunday the 6th of August 1810.

James M. Howell was born on Saturday the 23 of January 1813.

Craven Howell died January 14, 1887 aged 81 years 3 months & 1 day.

George and Mary Ann Holmes et al[4]
Quitclaim to Alfred Howell
15 March 1844

Know all men by these presents that we George Holmes and Mary Ann wife of said George Holmes, Robert Lyons and Margaret wife of said Robert Lyons, Samuel Pyle and Francis wife of said Samuel Pyle and James Howell and Eliza wife of said James Howell in consideration of the sum of twenty five dollars in hand paid by Alfred Howell (to each of us) do hereby remise release and forever quitclaim unto the said Alfred Howell his heirs and assigns forever all our title interest and estate legal and equitable in the following premises with the appurtenances situate in the County of Muskingum and State of Ohio It being the South west quarter of Section twenty six in township thirteen of Range Eleven containing one hundred and sixty three acres & twenty six hundredths of an acre of Lands directed to be sold at Zanesville (Ohio) In Testimony Whereof we have hereunto set our hands and seals this 15th day of March AD 1844.

Executed in presence of
Geo Johnson
Maria Bliany?
Mary Mowry
Jacob Mapel?
John J Carr

> George Holmes (seal)[5]
> Mary Ann x Holmes (seal)[6]
> Robert Lyons (seal)
> Margaret x Lyons (seal)[7]
> Samuel Pyle (seal)

---

[4] Muskingum County, OH, Deed Bk 18:453.

[5] George Holmes was the administrator for Abner Howell's estate.

[6] Mary Ann Howell married George Holmes, 8 March 1838.

[7] Margaret Howell married Robert Lyons, 9 April 1840.

Fanny Pyle (seal)[8]
James Howell (seal)
Eliza Howell (seal)
William Hyde (seal)
Ura x Hyde (seal)[9]

Holmes, Lyons, Pyles and Howell personally appeared in Muskingum County, 15 March 1844; Hydes personally appeared in Guernsey County, OH, 9 May 1844.

Entered: 16 December 1850
Recorded: 2 January 1851

---

[8] Frances Howell married Samuel Pyle, 1 May 1828.

[9] Urey Howell married William Hyde, 26 September 1833.

Abner Howell et al[10]
Deed to George Howell
18 January 1845

Know all men by these presents that we John Howell Abner Howell
and John Shamlin and Martha Shamlin his wife late Martha Howell
the said Martha being one of the heirs and daughter of Abner Howell
decd of the County of Muskingum in the State of Ohio for and in
consideration of the sum of Two Hundred and Twenty five dollars in
hand paid by George Howell of the County and State aforesaid the
receipt whereof we do hereby acknowledge have given granted
bargained sold conveyed and confirmed unto the said George Howell
his heirs and assigns forever all our right title interest claim and
demands at law and in Equity in and to the following described parcel
of land situate in said Muskingum County to wit it being the South
West quarter of section twenty six in township thirteen of Range
Eleven containing one hundred and Sixty three acres and twenty Six
hundredths of an acre Except forty acres sold of the North East corner
of said quarter to Alfred Howell.   To have and to hold the said
granted and bargained premises with all the appurtenances and
privileges to the same belonging or in anywise apertaining to the said
George Howell his heirs and assigns forever to his own propper his
benefit and behoof forever - in fee simple.   In witness whereof the
said parties have hereunto set their hands and seals this 18th day of
January AD 1845 -

Sined Sealed &	John Howell (seal)	Delivered
in	Abner Howell (seal)	
presence of	John x Shamlin (seal)	
James Carnes	Martha x Shamlin (seal)	
Andrew G. Carnes		

---

[10] Muskingum County, OH, Deed Bk 10:14.

The State of Ohio Muskingum County

I James Carnes an active Justice of the peace of said county do hereby certify that on this 18th day of January AD 1845 Personally appeared before me John Howell Abner Howell & John Shamlin and Martha his wife siners to the written deed and acknowledged the signing and sealing thereof to be their act and deed and at the same time the said Martha was examined by me seperate and apart from her said husband the said John Shamlin and the contents of said deed was by me made know to her She there acknowledged the signing and Sealing to be her volunteer act ??? Given under my hand the date before written.

James Carnes, J.P.

Entered Jan. 19th 1846
Recorded Jan. 28 1846

Muskingum County, Ohio Court Records[11]
April Term 1847

George Holmes, Administrator of the estate of Abner Howell, dec[d]

vs

Elizabeth Howell
John Shamlin & Martha Shamlin his wife
Alfred Howell
Alexander Grandstaff & Amanda Grandstaff his   wife
Robert Lyons & Margaret Lyons his wife
George Holmes and Mary Ann Holmes his wife
George Howell
James Howell

Petition to sell land
Petition filed April 17th 1847
subfr iss? same date returnable
forthwith. Returned "served" on all accept Alex Grandstaff & wife
not found, fees. 5.90

August Term, 1847, (S238) continued
Nov Term, 1847, (S364) con
April Term, 1848 (S481) con
June Term, 1848 (587) con
Sept Term, 1848 (T91) con
Feb Term, 1849 (235) con
June Term, 1849 (346) con
September Term, 1849 (T482) Bill dismissed at cost of Defendants,
by agreement.

---

[11] Muskingum County, OH, Court Records, Appointment Docket S, page 400, 1846-1848.

Alexander and Amanda Grandstaff[12]
Quitclaim to George Howell
27 April 1847

Know all men by these presents that we Alexander Grandstaff and Amanda Grandstaff[13] wife of said Alexander Grandstaff in consideration of the sum of Seventy five dollars to us in hand paid by George Howell do hereby remise release and forever quitclaim unto the said George Howell his heirs and assigns forever all our title interest and estate legal and equitable in the following premises with the appurtenances situate in Rich hill Township Muskingum County Ohio and bounded and described as follows All of one thirteenth undivided part of the South West quarter of Section Twenty Six in Township Thirteen of Range Eleven containing one hundred and Sixty three acres and Twenty Six hundredths of an acre Except forty acres of said land deeded to Alfred Howell and land owned by Abner Howell deceased late of Rich Hill Township - In testimony Whereof we have hereunto set our hands and seals this twenty seventh day of April in the year Eighteen Hundred and Forty Seven -

Signed in presence of
John McIntire
Sarah A. McIntire

                        Alexander Grandstaff (seal)
                        Amanda Grandstaff (seal)

Note: Grandstaffs appeared, Amanda examined separately, 27 April 1847

Entered: 5 June 1848
Recorded: 8 June 1848

---

[12] Muskingum County, OH, Deed Bk 13:7.

[13] Amanda Howell married Alexander Grandstaff, 16 May 1831.

Isabella Howell[14]
Quitclaim to William Cariens,
1 July 1847

Know all men by these presents that I Isabel Howell widow of Abner
Howell deceased of the County of Muskingum and State of Ohio in
consideration of the Sum of Sixty dollars in hand paid by William
Cariens of the county and State aforesaid do hereby remise release and
forever quit claim unto the said William Cariens his heirs and assigns
forever all our title interest and estate legal and Equitable in the
following premises with the appurtenances Situate in the County of
Muskingum and State of Ohio and bounded and described as follows
being a part of the South West qr of Section 26 Township 13 and
Range 11 beginning at the South West corner of Said qr thence N 1
degree E distance 22 chains to a post thence South 89 degrees 46' E
distance 21 chains to a post from which bears a poplar tree 30 inches
diameter S 5 degrees 30' E distance 13 links thence S 5 degrees 55'
E distance 22 chains 20 links to a Stone on the South line of said qr
thence N 89 degrees 46'West distance 23 chains and 36 links to the
place of beginning containing 48 acres and 80 hundredths.   In
testimony whereof I have hereunto set my hand and Seal this first day
of July one thousand eight hundred and Forty Seven.

Executed in presence of
John St. Clair
George Howell

                                          Isable x Howell (seal)[15]

---

[14] Muskingum County, OH, Deed Bk 13:6-7.

[15] In Abner's estate packet there is a statement of payment to George Johnson,
D S, from Abner Howell, dec., for "marrying him and making return of same," for
$1.50 and for "writing and acknowledging deed to Alfred Howell," for $.50. In
Muskingum County Ohio Marriages, 1835-1848, Book 3, there is a marriage
between Abner Howell and Isabella McCracken, 2 april 1841. Hence Isabella is not
Abner's first marriage and not the mother of his children.

The State of Ohio Muskingum County ss

Before me John St Clair a Justice of the peace in and for said County personally appeared the within named Isable Howell and acknowledge the signing and sealing of the within conveyance to be her Voluntary act and deed -

This 1st day of July AD 1847

John St Clair JP

Entered: 5 June 1848
Recorded:8 June 1848

Alfred and Sophrona E. Howell[16]
Quitclaim to George Howell
1 July 1847

Know all men by these presents That we Alfred Howell and Sophrona E Howell wife of said Alfred Howell of the County of Muskingum and State of Ohio in consideration of the Sum of Three Hundred Dollars in hand paid by George Howell of the County and State aforesaid do hereby remise release and forever quit claim unto the said George Howell his heirs and assigns forever all our title interest and estate legal and equitable in the following premises with the appurtenances situate in the county of Muskingum and state of Ohio and bounded and described as follows being a part of the South West qr Section 26 Township 13 and Range 11 beginning at the South West corner of said qr thence North 1 degree E distance 22 chaines to a post thence South 89 degrees 46' E distance 21 chains to a post from which bears a poplar tree 30 inches diameter S 5 degrees 20' E distance 13 links thence S 5 degrees 55' E distance 22 chains 20 links to a Stone on the South line of said qr thence North 89 degrees 46' W distance 23 chains and 36 links to the place of begining containing 48 acres and 80 hundredths In testimony whereof we have hereunto set our hands and seals this first day of July one thousand Eight hundred and forty seven.

Executed in presence of
George Cariens
John St. Clair

Alfred x Howell (seal)

Sofroany a Edna Howell (seal)

---

[16] Muskingum County, OH, Deed Bk 13:5.

Note: Alfred and Sophrona personally appeared, 1 July 1847.

Entered: 5 June 1848
Recorded: 8 June 1848

George and Martha Howell[17]
Quitclaim to William Cariens
1 July 1847

[Identical property described in Alfred and Sophrona Quitclaim.]

Entered: 5 June 1848
Recorded: 6 June 1848

---

[17] Muskingum County, OH, Deed Bk 13:6.

Joseph Kaler[18]
Deed to George Howell of Muskingum County
80 Acres in Hocking County, Ohio
30 August 1847

Know all men by these presents that Joseph Kaler and Leah Kaler the
County of Hocking and State of Ohio in consideration of the sum of
??? hundred dollars in hand paid by George Howell of the State of
Ohio and County of Muskingum have bargained and sold and do
hereby grant bargain sell and convey unto the said George Howell his
heirs and assigns forever, the following premises situate in the county
of Hocking in said State of Ohio and bounded and described as
follows: The East half of the South West quarter of Section No.
Twelve (12) of Township No. Twelve (12) of Range No. Seventeen
(17) containing Eighty acres more or less. To have and to hold, said
premises with the appurtenances unto the said George Howell his heirs
and assigns forever, and the said Joseph and Leah Kaler for
themselves and heirs do hereby covenant with said George Howell his
heirs and assigns that they are lawfully of the premises aforesaid, and
that the premises are free and clear of all encumbrances whatsoever,
and they will forever warrant and defend the same with the
appurtenances unto the said George Howell his heirs and assigns,
against the lawful claims of all persons whomsoever. In testimony
whereof, the said Joseph Kaler and Leah Kaler his wife have hereunto
set their hands and seals this 30th day of August in the year of our
Lord one thousand eight hundred and forty seven.

Signed Sealed and acknowledged in presence of us
Joel Gibson
Samuel Pyle

                                    Joseph Kaler (seal)
                                    Leah x Kaler (seal)

---

[18] Hocking County, OH, Deed Bk I:324.

The State of Ohio Hocking County ss

Before me Joel Gibson a Justice of the Peace, in and for said County personally appeared the above named Joseph Kaler and Leah Kaler his wife, and acknowledged the signing and sealing of the above conveyance to be their voluntary act and deed the said Leah Kaler being at the same time examined by me separate and apart from her said husband the contents of said instrument made known to her by me she then declares that she did voluntarily sign seal and acknowledge the same, and that she is still satisfied therewith this 30th day of August A.D. 1847.

Recorded Sept. 8 1847

> J. Gibison J.P.
> B. Hersh Recr.

George and Martha Howell[19]
Deed to James Lee
80 Acres in Swan Township, Vinton County, Ohio
27 November 1863

Know all Men by These presents that We George Howell and Martha Howell wife of Said George Howell of the County of Vinton and State of Ohio In Consideration of the Sum of Eleven Hundred ($1100.00) Dollars in hand paid by James Lee of the County of Vinton and state of Ohio Have bargained and Sold and do hereby Grant Bargain Sell and Convey unto the Said James Lee and unto his heirs and assigns forever the following real estate Situated in the County of Vinton and State of Ohio and bounded and Described as follows to wit. The East half of the South west quarter of Section Number twelve (12) of Township Number twelve (12) of Range Number Seventeen (17) Containing Eighty acres More or less. To Have and to Hold Said premises with the appurtenances unto the Said James Lee and unto his heirs and assigns forever And the Said George Howell and Martha Howell his wife for their heirs executors and administrators doth hereby Covenant with the Said James Lee and with his heirs and assigns that they are lawfully Seized(?) of the premises aforesaid that the premises are free and clear of all encumbrances whatsoever and that they Will forever Warrant and Defend the Same with the appurtenances unto the Said James Lee, and unto his heirs and assigns against the lawful Claims of all persons whomsoever. In Testimony thereof the Said George Howell and Martha Howell his wife have hereunto Set their hand and Seals on this Twenty Seventh Day of 27th Day of November A.D. 1863.

Executed in presence of

Isaac Reynolds   George Howell (seal)
Daniel Shurtz   Martha x Howell (seal)

---

[19] Vinton County, OH, Deed Bk 9:319. Vinton County was formed in 1850, partly from Hocking County.

The State of Ohio
Vinton County SS

Before me Isaac Reynolds the undersigned a justice of the Peace within and for Said County personally appeared George Howell and acknowledged the Signing and Sealing of the foregoing Conveyance to be their voluntary act and Deed. And the Said Martha Howell being at the Same time Examined by me Separate and apart from her Said husband & the Contents of said Deed made known to her by me She then Declared that She did voluntarily Sign Seal and Acknowledge the Same and that She is Still Satisfied therewith

In Testimony Whereof I hereunto subscribe my Name and affix my Seal officially at Swan Township Vinton County Ohio this 27 Day of November A.D. 1863.

Isaac Reynolds Justice of Peace (seal)
Jonathan Brine

Entered: 29 December 1863
Recorded: 29 December 1863

Appendix B

Census Records

CENSUS RECORDS

Census records are probably one of the most helpful of tools in tracing family history ... at least for the period between 1790 and 1920. This was certainly true in the case of these Howells. Beginning as we did with Abner[3] Howell and working in both directions, we relied heavily on census information to lead us in both directions ... back to Virginia and forward to show how the family began to spread out and away from Muskingum County. We have included a couple of census records in the body of this report. Other census records considered "key" in helping us following these Howells are presented here. We were able to find 10 of Abner's 13 children in the 1850 census records, the first year all members of the household were listed by name. All of Abner's sons were listed as farmers, which was pretty typical for this period of time. Even the daughters all married farmers, with the exception of Amanda, whose husband, Alexander Grandstaff, was a shoemaker.

Table 3. James Howell Household, Highland Township, Muskingum County, Ohio, 1850

Page	Name	Age	Occupation	Birth Place
422	James	45	farmer	VA
	Eliza	29		OH
	John F.	5		OH

Table 4. Alfred Howell Household, Rich Hill
Township, Muskingum County, Ohio, 1850

Page	Name	Age	Occupation	Birth Place
484	Alfred	46	farmer	VA
	Safronia	34		NC
	Wm	18	farmer	OH
	Sarah A.	16		OH
	James W.?	14	farmer	OH
	George	13		OH
	Mary A.	7		OH
	Alfred	4		OH
	John	2		OH
	Madison	24	laborer	OH

Table 5. John Shamlin Household, Perry Township
Muskingum County, Ohio, 1850

Page	Name	Age	Occupation	Birth Place
480	John	70	farmer	VA
	Martha	42		VA
	Alfred	22	farmer	OH
	Aaron	20	laborer	OH
	French	18	laborer	OH
	Mary A.	13		OH
	Frances	9		OH

Table 6. Samuel Pyles Household, Swan Township
Vinton County, Ohio, 1850

Page	Name	Age	Occupation	Birth Place
654	Samuel	59	farmer	PA
	Frances A.	38		VA
	William	20	farmer	OH
	Isac?	17	farmer	OH
	Samuel	16	farmer	OH

Table 7. Alexander Grandstaff Household,
Benton Township, Hocking County, Ohio, 1850

Page	Name	Age	Occupation	Birth Place
437	Alexander	44	shoemaker	
	Amamda	41		VA
	Mary	17		OH
	Martha A.	15		OH
	Joseph	13		OH
	Ura	11		OH
	Julian	9		OH
	John	5		OH
	Hannah F.	4		OH
	Amanda M.	1		OH
	George Medln?	12		NJ

Table 8. George Holmes Household, Hopewell
Township, Muskingum County, Ohio, 1850

Page	Name	Age	Occupation	Birth Place
88	George	46	farmer	VA
	Mary Ann	34		VA
	Elizabeth Redman	12		OH

Table 9. George Howell Household, Swan
Township, Vinton County, Ohio, 1850

Page	Name	Age	Occupation	Birth Place
654	George	32	farmer	VA
	Martha	31		OH
	Mary	9		OH
	Eliza	7		OH
	James	5		OH
	Sarah	4		OH
	John	2		OH
	Alfred	8/12		OH

Table 10. Robert Lyons Household, Rich Hill Township,
Muskingum County, Ohio, 1850

Page	Name	Age	Occupation	Birth Place
480	Robert	31	farmer	PA
	Margaret	32		OH
	John	9		OH
	Elizabeth	7		OH
	William	6		OH
	Andrew	5		OH
	Jane	3		OH
	James	2		OH

Table 11. Abner Howell Household, Knox Township, Guernsey
County, Ohio, 1850

Page	Name	Age	Occupation	Birth Place
480	Abner	27	farmer	OH
	Louisa	23		OH
	Elizabeth	5		OH
	James H.	3		OH
	Sarah	6/12		OH

INDEX